DATE DUE

SUBJECT TO OVERDUE FINES
CALL ~~476-4260~~ TO RENEW

Pilgrimage

For my godchildren

Pilgrimage

David Souden

Quest Books
Theosophical Publishing House

Wheaton, Illinois ♦ Chennai (Madras), India

The Theosophical Society wishes to acknowledge the generous support of the Kern Foundation in the publication of this book.

Text copyright © 2001 by The Ivy Press

First Quest Edition 2001
Copublished with The Ivy Press 2001

The Theosophical Publishing House
P. O. Box 270
Wheaton, IL 60189-0270

Library of Congress Cataloging-in-Publication Data
Souden, David.
Pilgrimage: twenty journeys to inspire the soul /
David Souden.
    p. cm.
ISBN 0-8356-0804-2
1. Pilgrims and pilgrimages.   I. Title.

BL619.P5 S68 2001
291.3'51—dc21   2001020269

This book was conceived, designed, and produced by The Ivy Press Limited
The Old Candlemakers, West Street
Lewes, East Sussex BN7 1UP

Creative Director: Peter Bridgewater
Publisher: Sophie Collins
Art Director: Tony Seddon
Editorial Director: Steve Luck
Designer: John Grain
Senior Project Editor: April McCroskie
Editor: Mike Darton
Picture Researcher: Vanessa Fletcher

Quest Substantive Editor: Sharron Dorr

Printed and bound in China

10 9 8 7 6 5 4 3 2 1

QUEST BOOKS are published by
The Theosophical Society in America,
Wheaton, Illinois, 60189-0270, a branch of a
world fellowship, a membership organization
dedicated to the promotion of the unity of
humanity and the encouragement of the study of
religion, philosophy, and science, to the end that
we may better understand ourselves and our place
in the universe. The Society stands for complete
freedom of individual search and belief. For
further information about its activities, write, call
1-800-669-1571, e-mail olcott@theosmail.net or
consult its Web page: http://www.theosophical.org

Contents

Pilgrimage as spiritual search

The largest gatherings anywhere in the world have been religious gatherings where bands of pilgrims congregate, whether they be Hindus at the Kumbh Mela in Allahabad, Muslims at Mecca, or Catholic Christians in Rome or Lourdes. To go on pilgrimage is one of the oldest-known religious activities in the story of humankind. Indeed, we have evidence that prehistoric people sometimes journeyed significant distances to their sacred sites—Stonehenge, say, or Carnac—and that they venerated sacred objects there. And pilgrimage is still one of the most characteristic aspects of religious life today. Even Protestant Christian denominations, which usually frown upon the practice, commonly regard life itself as a metaphorical pilgrimage.

A pilgrimage is foremost a journey in which one leaves home to travel—whether a short or a long distance—to a sacred site. Yet a pilgrimage is much more. As pilgrims, travelers encounter rituals, holy objects and sacred architecture. They may travel alone or in groups, the experience of which may be as important as achieving any individual goal. Sometimes the journey itself is the essential aspect of the pilgrimage, involving hardship and requiring physical strength. At other times, the journey is almost immaterial, and the destination is all—as now modern transportation so frequently makes possible. Pilgrimage may also be as much about returning home with one's memories and souvenirs as it is about having reached the destination.

Pilgrimage serves various purposes. It may, for instance, be a rite of passage, as it is for the elderly Greek Orthodox who go to Jerusalem to prepare for death. Or it may be a quest for a goal that transcends life, as it is for Hindus who bathe in the sacred waters of the Ganges in the hope of escaping the eternal round of death and rebirth. On the other hand, pilgrimage may be the occasion for reflection, as it is for Buddhists who contemplate the inner self while sitting in a Kyoto temple garden. Pilgrimage may offer a heightened sense of solidarity and community, as it does for Muslims

when they perform the *hajj*—the annual journey to Mecca that is one of the building blocks of their faith. Particular pilgrimages, such as the one to the Czarna Madonna in the town of Czestochowa, may even underline national and nationalist outlooks and sympathies. And pilgrimages may promise the healing of physical or spiritual ills, whether it be from the waters of the Marian shrine at Lourdes or from the ancient earth spirit of Kataragama in Sri Lanka that appeals simultaneously to Christians, Muslims, Buddhists, and Hindus.

The pages that follow describe twenty pilgrim routes and sites around the world. Some are small and local; others are global in their reach and appeal. Some are sites of great antiquity; others may be recent or new. Some routes entail suffering and hardship; on others, the way may be easy. Whatever the circumstances, whatever the religion, our purpose here is to celebrate pilgrimage as a basic form of human activity that has had spiritual meaning for all manner of people and all varieties of faith, now and throughout time.

Saddhus, *Hindu holy men, lead pilgrims in their millions down to the steps on the banks of the Ganges, and there they all bathe at the sacred spot where the amrit fell.*

Allahabad and the Kumbh Mela

THE KUMBH MELA (or Kumba Mela) is the greatest religious show on earth. Indeed, it may be the greatest show on earth of any kind. On February 6, 1989, an estimated fifteen million pilgrims traveled to Allahabad, in the north Indian state of Uttar Pradesh, on the occasion of the full Kumbh Mela. They comprised some three percent of the entire Hindu population of India. According to The Guinness Book of Records, *this gathering was then the "greatest recorded number of human beings assembled with a common purpose in history."*

ABOVE: *In spite of the crush of so many people, for the pilgrim the Kumbh offers a crucial step toward individual immortality.*

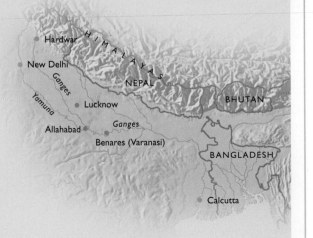

9

In January 2001, when the Hindu sacred festival was again held in Allahabad after the traditional twelve-year interval, the numbers were greater than ever before. This time it was an even holier and more auspicious occasion—one that would only happen every twelve times twelve, or 144 years. The authorities were expecting forty million people, although the numbers probably rose to seventy million. All these people come to bathe in the sacred rivers that meet at this holy place. They hope thereby to achieve enlightenment and release from the otherwise eternal cycle of rebirths that is one of the basic tenets of Hindu belief.

SACRED WATERS

A riverside religious festival, the Kumbh Mela is held every three years, rotating between Hardwar on the River Ganges in the Himalayan foothills, Ujjain on the River Sipra in central India, Nasik on the River Godavari near Mumbai (Bombay) in the west and—most significant of them all—at Allahabad, also known as Prayag, which stands in north-central India at the confluence of the Ganges, the Yamuna, and the mythical underground Saraswati rivers. Allahabad is to Hindus what Mecca is to Muslims, what Bodh Gaya (where the Buddha found enlightenment) is to Buddhists, and what Rome and Jerusalem are to many Christians. All the sins relating to a Hindu's former lives and to the present life begin to "tremble like a tree struck by a great wind" when he or she embarks on a pilgrimage to the Kumbh Mela.

Each of these four cities therefore hosts the festival every dozen years. Six years after each full Kumbh there is a half-Kumbh Mela in both

RIGHT: The pilgrim millions come to adore Mother Ganges, the source of life and the most sacred of India's rivers. For each kumbh, vast tent cities are erected with all the services a permanent city would require.

ABOVE: A pilgrim seeks immortality and an end to the otherwise endless cycle of reincarnated lives by bathing in the river at the most auspicious time and in a place that will bring him the greatest grace.

Hardwar and Allahabad, which attracts smaller but still sizeable crowds. The 2001 festival that took place in Allahabad, the greatest of the four, was an event of which nobody will see its like again in his or her lifetime.

Millions of pilgrims from every corner of the Indian subcontinent, and from much further afield, descend on the appointed town at the appointed time, usually in January or February. They come from the big cities—Delhi, Calcutta, and Mumbai (Bombay)—or from the desert villages of Rajasthan and settlements on the western coast. They speak different languages, they bear different and distinct marks on their foreheads denoting which religious sect they belong to, they wear different types of clothing, and they observe separate customs. But they all meet to immerse themselves in the sacred waters of these rivers. No general invitation is given, no formal advertising is done (at least within India), and no single religious authority oversees it all. Yet people know where and when to come, setting off from their far-flung villages and cities.

The climax of the pilgrimage comes on an astrologically significant date, when Jupiter is in the constellation we know as Aquarius and the sun enters Aries. *Kumbh* is the Sanskrit name for "Aquarius"—the Latin name of which is generally translated as "water-carrier," but can alternatively

mean "water-container." Mela is ordinarily translated as "fair" or "festival." The Kumbh *Mela* gets its
name from Aquarius not as the carrier, but as the
container—the jar (*kumba*) of nectar (*amrit*) in
Hindu mythology. At the beginning of time, it is
said, the gods and demons together churned the
ocean made of milk to extract an elixir which
would confer immortality (Hindi *amrit* is cognate
with Latin–English *immort-*). Although the gods
had agreed to share this elixir with the demons,
they absconded with the jar. They fled over the
course of twelve days—twelve days for the gods
equal twelve human years—and the amrit spilled
on these four places on Earth: Allahabad, Hardwar,
Ujjain, and Nasik. Allahabad is twice blessed, since
another story of the gods records that it was also

*ABOVE: Special pilgrim trains bring worshippers vast distances from
across the subcontinent to the site of the Kumbh Mela. Their journeys
may take days, and the crush will be just as great when they arrive.*

the place that a single drop of Shiva's semen fell to
earth—another key to immortality.

The River Ganges is, for all Hindus, the most
sacred of waterways. These are the waters of the
mother goddess Ganga, flowing from the
Himalayan mountains across the plains to the Bay
of Bengal. To bathe in them, to make private devotions, and to recite the sacred invocations to the
deities is to be blessed. Besides the festivals of the
Kumbh Mela, the most sacred site is at Benares (or
Varanasi), fifty miles (eighty kilometers) from
Allahabad and a town celebrated throughout the

Wearing garlands of marigolds and with their bodies and hair smeared in ashes, the saddhus who usually live in solitary austerity will only meet as a group at the Kumbh Mela.

world for the scale of Hindu pilgrimage. It is particularly holy to be cremated on the banks of the Ganges and to have one's ashes scattered on the river, or even for the corpse to be floated into the river to sink into the muddy bottom. The ashes of Mahatma Gandhi, the founder of modern India, were scattered on the rivers' point of confluence at Allahabad, making this a semisecular pilgrimage destination for some Indians.

RENOUNCING THE WORLD

Particularly prominent among the religious groups that return to the Kumbh every twelve years are holy men who have renounced the worldly life and who travel naked or near-naked, without any possessions. Their whole lives are spent as religious pilgrims, moving from one holy place to another, celebrating the particular deities they worship through their ascetic way of life. Some are devotees of Krishna or Shiva, others of Vishnu or other gods and manifestations of the preeminent deities.

On the main bathing days these holy men, known in general as *saddhus*, lead the millions of pilgrims in a parade from the camp down to the *ghat* (stepped landing place) on the Ganges. At the head of this procession are always *nagas*, a particular order of ascetics dedicated to Shiva. In the Kumbh procession many of the nagas march naked. They claim to be particularly resolute defenders of the Hindu community and have led the processions for many centuries. Some groups of nagas display their skill in wrestling or in the use of swords and other weapons.

Pilgrims endeavor to bathe in the Ganges at precisely the spot where the amrit fell, on the anniversary of that event. They hope by doing so to take a step toward immortality. Allahabad is especially significant because of its position at the confluence of the three sacred rivers. Pilgrims believe that

bathing and praying there generates a spiritual energy. Thousands of aspirants take advantage of what they regard as that energy to commit themselves to the renunciate's intense religious practice, becoming holy men themselves, and thus contributing to the collective consciousness through personal purification.

THE PRESS OF HUMANITY

Most pilgrims to the Mela site find themselves accommodated in tents on the ground with hundreds of thousands of their fellow seekers after divine truth and enlightenment. Cooking, eating, sleeping, and personal hygiene are all conducted in the same tight quarters. Being robbed is a constant threat, especially for Westerners. So is disease. Violence has often broken out between different factions and religious groups. The better-off may choose to stay in a hotel, and the cities' accommodations agencies brace themselves for their twelve-yearly invasion as best they can. Flights from Oregon, Pennsylvania, or Germany bring their own pilgrim bands, who usually opt for the greater comfort of hotel living. The search for spirituality from other non-Western religions has helped swell the number of attendees further still.

Among the millions of people, only a few thousand come out of sheer curiosity, as tourists, reporters, photographers, or filmmakers. They usually choose to focus on sensational aspects such as the naked saddhus and drug-crazed holy men. For these spectators the Kumbh Mela is a spectacle, but within the Kumbh Mela as a whole exists the full spectrum of Hindu religious activities. Elaborate trade exhibits market the wares of India's major companies. Nonprofit charitable organizations advertise their presence. Artists, craftsmen, entertainers, *swamis* (Hindu male religious teachers), priests, astrologers, fortune-tellers, and

The Master of Fire. The extreme ascetic practices the West frequently associates with Hinduism, such as fire walking and body piercing, are integral parts of the festival observance.

ABOVE: Naga saddhus—all followers of one particular guru or teacher—ride in procession to the water's edge. Elaborate floats also carry effigies of Lord Shiva and other deities past devout spectators.

beggars all press on the faithful for their attention. Police are in evidence everywhere. They direct traffic, since many more pilgrims now come by car and bus as well as the traditional means—on foot and then by train. Above all, the police keep order. For all the spirituality of the occasion, petty crime is rife and tempers flare. At the 1998 Kumbh Mela at Hardwar, paramilitary forces were called in to curb rioting that broke out in certain quarters.

Yet inside the tens of thousands of tents pitched away from the accessible and "glamorous" spots along the main roads, millions of people engage—unseen except by their neighbors—in acts of charity and kindness, in fasting, meditation, and reciting the scriptures. Many are there for a month-long study in the company of religious teachers. Many others come to the towns of the Kumbh Mela for their own life-cycle rituals, often accompanied by priests who may have served their families for generations. Flowers are cast upon the waters as well as bodies immersed in it. There are those who will even have made the journey with the corpses of their loved ones in order to cremate them at the water's edge; and others will bring cremation ashes, bones, or even personal effects of the dead to place in the sacred waters.

HARDWAR

The population of the small town of Hardwar in northern India was swollen to almost breaking point when the estimated ten million pilgrims arrived in 1998 to bathe in the Ganges. The town is sometimes also called *Ganga-dvar* (door of the Ganges) since it is regarded as the place where the river leaves the Himalayan mountains to begin its long journey across the plains to the Bay of Bengal. It is also often the starting point for pilgrims proceeding further to religious centers in the mountains: the Kumbh Mela itself is only the biggest and best-known event in a complex ritual system in the locality.

Hardwar has been a pilgrim's destination at least since the time of the great Buddhist traveler Hsuan Tsang (who left China bound for India in 629). Contemporary pilgrims tend to regard the Kumbh Mela as a pilgrimage event that has been reenacted since time immemorial, but the earliest written reference dates the gathering there to the early sixteenth century. The coming of the railroad to Hardwar in the mid 1880s allowed much more convenient access to the town for pilgrims. An estimated crowd of one million people attended the Kumbh Mela in 1938, and the event has grown in scale ever since.

The holy men attending the Kumbh Mela always have their own bases, separate from the other pilgrims. At Hardwar, the *Vairagi* camp—devotees of Vishnu—lies far to the south of the town. The other two groups of saddhus at the Kumbh Mela, the *sannyasis* (worshippers of Shiva) and the *udasis* (who are actually Sikhs), own property in Hardwar and the surrounding area, so their camps are right in town near their permanent *ashrams* (religious retreats).

The pilgrims' camps are situated on a chain of otherwise uninhabited islands in the flood plain of the Ganges, connected to the town by a series of bridges. Some of these bridges are permanent, others are erected for the Mela and are dismantled when it is over. Most camps have a ceremonial gateway made of colored cloth stretched over a wooden frame. A sign identifies the group whose camp it is and often names the swami who is the head of the group. The typical camp includes a *pandal*, a large open tent for public meetings. Electricity is supplied (for a modest fee) by the Mela Administration and it is needed not only for lighting, but also to power the public-address system. The services at each camp are broadcast to those assembled there and to passersby. People sleep overnight under canvas—if the loudspeakers of the surrounding camps allow them any rest.

TIME IN FLUX

The festival of Kumbh Mela brings millions upon millions of believers to Allahabad and its three partner towns in turn. It also reminds Hindus that time is cyclical. *Samsara*, the Hindu notion of a never-ending life cycle, is central to the beliefs of all those who come to bathe in the sacred waters. The round of events is governed by astrological principles and an unyielding calendar. Above all, what exists must dissolve and reappear. The lucky ones will achieve immortality there and not have to go through the eternal round of rebirth and new incarnations any more.

Looking down from a first floor window, pilgrims to the Golden Temple find themselves in a place of rich magnificence that has withstood many onslaughts over three centuries.

JOURNEY TWO

Amritsar and the Golden Temple

THEIR EYES SPARKLING beneath their immaculate white turbans, the smiling tour operators beam from the pages of the travel brochures sent out by their agencies in the Punjab. Received in Canada, Australia, Britain, South Africa, and other parts of India and Pakistan, the brochures assure travelers that their every need will be met on their pilgrimage to Amritsar, which is the primary destination for all Sikhs. They have been coming to Amritsar for more than four hundred years, and for the past three centuries their principal objective among the gold-leafed splendor and limpid waters of the temple complex has been a bound set of manuscript pages.

ABOVE: *A pilgrim wears the turban that is a true mark of Sikhism.*

21

The Sikhs, the religious group centered in the Punjab in northwest India, emerged in the course of the sixteenth century. With their characteristic turbans and full beards, and their warrior traditions, Sikhs have a special place in the history of Indian religion. Theirs has been a troubled history in which torrents of blood have been spilled. The Sikhs were also among the first Indian communities to begin large-scale emigration from India to other parts of the world—first to Canada at least a century ago, subsequently to Britain and other countries. Sikhism does not actively seek converts, but its adherents are often very fervent in their beliefs. Whether they live in Toronto or Wolverhampton, Lahore or Rawalpindi, Sikhs want to visit the temple complex at Amritsar at least once. There they will meditate upon their troubled and martial history and venerate their *Guru*: a book set under a canopy upon a silk cushion.

SIKHISM AND THE RELIGIONS OF INDIA

Pilgrimage is integral to all the religions of India. Jains are ever on the move—the pilgrims' pilgrims. Hindus, Buddhists, Sikhs, and Muslims all consider pilgrimage to be sacred duties. The religions that stem from India itself—Jainism, Hinduism, Buddhism, and Sikhism—share a ritual vocabulary of bathing, the scattering of flowers, and ideas of purity; and each has a fundamental notion of *dharma*, moral spiritual goals. There are also essential differences: one god or many gods, a defined or an undefinable deity.

Of these religions, Sikhism is certainly distinctive. Nanak, its founding Guru, emphasized piety and devotion, rejecting caste, magic, and miracles

RIGHT: *The Baba Gujhaji tree in the temple complex is 450 years old, the survivor from the forest clearing where the first gurus sat to meditate beside the pool that now encircles the Golden Temple itself.*

ABOVE: Reading from the Granth Sahib, the sacred text of the Sikhs that was the last and the supreme Guru. The ceremonies surrounding it are at the very heart of the temple activities at Amritsar.

in the search for the One God. Nanak was born near Lahore in 1496, and the Punjab was, and remains, the heartland of the Sikh religion. He traveled to holy places throughout the Indian subcontinent, developing a theology of the One God (even if that deity had many names) and rejecting the caste distinctions of Hinduism. After his death a succession of Gurus followed him, all refining the theology and extending the body of sacred writings. The "Five Ks"—adopted at the end of the seventeenth century for all Sikh men who wish to be among the *Khalsa* (pure ones)—directly contradict

tenets of Hinduism. The Ks are *kes*, uncut hair; *kanga*, the comb that holds it beneath the turban; *kirpan*, the sword, with *kara*, the steel bracelet that controls it; and the *kacch*, a loincloth that shrouds an uncircumcised penis. Traditionally men are given the surname *Singh* (lion), while women are given *Gaur* (princess.)

THE SIKH SHRINE

The Golden Temple began with the third Guru, Amar Das, who used to meditate beside a pool of water 160 kilometres (100 miles) east of Lahore. His successor, Guru Ram Das, nominated in 1574, chose to live there. This was to be where the House of God, the Harmandir Sahib, would be built and

Sumptuously attired and with a gaze of steel, this nihang or priest from the Golden Temple guards the sacred treasures that Sikh pilgrims come from across the world to behold.

around which Amritsar grew. Its name means "pool of nectar" or "water of immortality." Succeeding Gurus embellished the site, first building a bathing tank and a simple brick temple in the center of the pool, but an important feature from the outset was that the temple had four doors, open equally to the four principal Hindu castes.

At the start of the seventeenth century it was decided that the complex was forever to be the repository of Sikh learning. The manuscript book of the Sikh scriptures, known as the *Granth Sahib*, was ceremonially installed in the new Golden Temple in 1604. Every day since then (emergencies excepted), it has been ceremonially brought there from its overnight resting place in the Katha Sahib. The last living Guru, Gobind Singh, who died in 1708, nominated the *Granth Sahib*, as the next, the last, and the supreme Guru.

MARTIAL LAWS

Militant Sikhs today want an independent homeland, Khalistan. The Golden Temple is an icon of their long struggle. First the Muslim Mughal emperors waged bloody war against them. The Sikhs fought back and an initially peaceful religion was transformed into a fighting faith.

In 1763 the Afghans occupied and destroyed the Temple. When the Sikhs regained control over the Punjab they decided to rebuild their shrine on a grander scale. An ever-growing throng of pilgrims was coming to see the Holy Book. In 1922 the Colonial Office handed the keys back to the Sikhs after almost a century of British guardianship, following the massacre at Jallianwallah Bagh in 1919, close to the Golden Temple. Troops under the command of Brigadier General Dyer gunned down unarmed people attending a mass prayer and political meeting. For Mahatma Gandhi, this signified the beginning of the end of British rule.

More than fifty years later, when Indira Gandhi was returned to power in 1977 after earlier declaring martial law, she sought to curb the power of militant Sikhism wanting independence for the Punjab. When an outspoken Sikh priest, together with leading dissidents, sought sanctuary in the Golden Temple, "Operation Blue Star" began. In June 1984, Indian Army tanks rolled in; five thousand civilians died and the Temple was badly damaged. Shortly after, Mrs. Gandhi was assassinated by her two Sikh bodyguards. A bloody wave of anti-Sikh violence followed.

TEMPLE RITUAL

Sikhism's militant tendency is in general restricted to a zealous minority, but the attraction of the Golden Temple is felt by all Sikhs. For thousands of pilgrims and the devout of Amritsar, the day begins at 3:00 A.M., preparing for a predawn visit. Outside its main entrance, the pilgrims (predominantly but far from exclusively men) remove their shoes and wash their feet; many stop to buy garlands of marigolds to take as offerings.

Descending the marble stairs to the *parkarma*, the marble path around the pool, they gaze across to the gold-clad Harmandir Sahib. The waters around it have a glassy stillness. Bowing low, worshippers then turn left to walk around the entire parkarma, stopping at shrines on the way, often bathing at the steps beside a particular shrine, before reaching the Harmandir. The military tradition is far from forgotten. The names of Sikh martyrs and soldiers who have died in battle are inscribed on marble plaques.

Even at this hour, worshippers fill the large space to capacity. These predawn pilgrims then witness the ritual of bearing the book, the *Guru Granth Sahib*, from the Katha Sahib to the Harmandir Sahib. The *palki*, a gold and silver palanquin, is prepared. Deep, resonant drumbeats sound as the chief priest appears carrying the *Guru Granth Sahib* on a cushion on his head. Throwing fragrant rose petals and chanting its praises, worshippers make way for the palki. The short passage across the causeway sometimes takes half an hour.

The high priest carries the *Guru* to its place of honor in the Harmandir, seats himself in front of the *Guru Granth Sahib*, ceremonially opens it, and reads aloud the *Vaq*, the Lord's message for the day. *Shabads*, the singing and reciting of sacred verses, continues all day and into the evening. Pilgrims always take away with them memories of the music and hymn singing that permeate the temple.

The worshippers step out of the Harmandir, walk around the inner parkarma to continue their observances at individual shrines before returning over the causeway. Pilgrims making this circuit vary from the elderly and infirm to newlyweds who have come to seek blessings for the life that lies ahead—brides in their scarlet and gold wedding dresses, grooms in crisply tied pink or red turbans. This pattern continues throughout the day. As the sun sets, and the walkers finish their round, the prayers end, the *Guru Granth Sahib* is reverentially closed, wrapped in fresh layers of silk and muslin, and carried back on the palki to the Katha Sahib for the night. The Temple's massive silver and rosewood doors close, and volunteers start the ritual cleansing of the shrine with milk and water.

In a few hours the doors will open again, and a new set of pilgrims will breathe in the serenity that they still find within the battle-scarred, crowded, and holy Golden Temple of Amritsar.

BELOW: *Deep in prayer at a shrine within the temple complex, this pilgrim has carefully arranged the garland of saffron and white flowers that he has brought here as an offering.*

A young Zuñi man wears the traditional jewelry and colorful costume for the ceremonies that have been integral to his pueblo since long before the Spaniards arrived.

Corn Mountain and the Zuñi Pueblo

WHEN THE ENGLISH novelist D. H. Lawrence reached New Mexico in 1922, he decided that his "savage pilgrimage" was finally over. He had rambled the world looking for a powerful precivilized culture, and in New Mexico he believed he had found it. It was the only place, he declared, that had ever changed him from the outside. Many other people, then and since, have come to New Mexico to discover anew the ancient wisdom it has to offer.

Visitors today to New Mexico discover that the principal cultural survivals have been the native people and the landscape they have refashioned. One tribe of native people offers a view of traditional behavior in which journeys are integral to ceremonial worship—the Zuñi.

PUEBLO PEOPLES

The incursion of the Navajo from the north and the arrival of the Spanish profoundly curtailed the destiny of the Hopi and the Zuñi Native American groups indigenous to the Southwest. Yet enough of them survived to ensure that their culture remained viable. For the most part, today the Zuñi live in a *pueblo* (settlement) on the Zuñi Reservation near the town of Zuñi in western New Mexico. They constitute in themselves a distinct family linguistically, although in their physical appearance, culture, and social organization they closely resemble other local Native Americans such as the Hopi. The pueblos are specially built villages that use adobe (mud-brick) as the principal construction material within the stout stone and mortar walls that encircle them.

Present-day Zuñi are descended from the inhabitants of the seven Zuñi towns discovered in 1539 by the Franciscan missionary Marcos de Niza and called by the Spanish the Seven Cities of Cíbola. Although de Niza had seen only one of the villages from a distance, it had been bathed in the golden rays of the setting sun, with the result that he reported that the Zuñi were possessed of immense quantities of gold. In 1540 the Spanish explorer Francisco Vásquez de Coronado led an expedition to find the fabulous Seven Cities. He conquered the Zuñi—but found no treasure. A Christian mission was established among them in 1629, to be dedicated to Our Lady of Guadalupe, but the Zuñi clung to their traditional beliefs. In 1680, when

ABOVE: *In a sequence of ceremonies devoted to the rain god, the sun, and the Great Spirit, the Kachina dancers of the pueblo people mark the passage of the seasons and invoke the blessings of the spirits.*

they numbered about 2,500, the Zuñi joined the successful Pueblo uprising against the Spanish, only to be subjugated by them again in 1692. (The Mexicans replaced the Spanish when the Zuñi became independent in 1821—and then in 1848 the territory was sold to the United States.)

Like the Hopi, the Zuñi are famed for their weaving and basketry, as well as for their turquoise jewelry. A Zuñi legend tells the story of the parrot and the crow, each of whom presents an egg to the Zuñi women, for them to decide which one they will keep. The women choose the egg of the crow

Corn Mountain, sacred focus of the midsummer pilgrimage of the Zuñi people, is the centerpiece of the ceremonies that are designed to ensure that rains will come to make the corn grow.

Portrayed playing his flute, the creator figure Awonawilona is a central figure in the cosmology of many Native American peoples of the southwestern United States.

because of its wonderful turquoise color. The Zuñi love of color is seen everywhere in their daily lives, their ceremonies, and even in the exquisite jewelry they produce, fashioned from turquoise, shell, and jet and set in silver with intricate inlaid patterns. Zuñi craftsworkers also carve animal images from translucent shell. Although the Zuñi do not make much pottery, they do have a tradition of beautiful work in clay and still use pots in their ceremonies.

FARMING AND THE GODS

Today, the Zuñi remain a strong nation, their population numbering around nine thousand. They farm the arid soil of the region using traditional irrigation methods. A tightly organized priestly group exercises great power over the tribe, which is divided into six groups (representing north, south, east, west, up, and down). Each group has its own *kiva* or ceremonial chamber, for although they were converted to Christianity long ago, the Zuñi also have a strong and enduring attachment to ancient religious rituals that are tied closely to the changing seasons and include special devotion to the rain god. Their most important crop is corn—a food plant that the Native Americans have perfected over millennia. Corn needs sunshine, which New Mexico usually has in abundance, and water, which is often desperately lacking. Although the Zuñi pueblo is built close to the Zuñi River, it is frequently dry: this area has on average less than ten inches (twenty-five centimeters) of rain a year. Hence the emphasis on ceremonies to bring the rain and to keep the sun shining.

A broad pantheon of spirit gods is common to all southwestern tribes. The hermaphroditic/androgynous supreme being of the Zuñi is Awonawilona, Creator of Life. The sun is the Heart of the Sky and the earth is the Corn Maiden. The moon and the principal stars are also deities. Koloowisi, the plumed serpent, is symbolized by lightning and associated with fertility, because lightning storms bring rain to the desert.

Most of the important Zuñi ceremonials are connected with the solstices, the longest and the shortest days of the year. The first of the two great rain dances is held in June in the belief that if the sun fails to turn in its annual course the community will be jeopardized because the crops will fail. The Pueblo Indians of New Mexico run relay races at the midsummer solstice—the longest day—to help give the sun strength at the start of its journey toward its winter home. The Zuñi have dedicated sky watchers who carefully observe the heavens to determine the dates for the ritual.

So once a year the Zuñi take their ceremonies outside the confines of the pueblo and journey some twenty miles (thirty-two kilometers) to Corn Mountain. Some venture there on horseback but most now have pickup trucks to get around. Families make a day of it, bringing the very old and the very young. Corn Mountain has, as its name implies, a central position in the tribal cosmology. If the mountain and its ruling gods are not visited, if the rain dances are not performed, and if the sky-watching ceremonies are not observed, the prospects for the corn crop are poor. Corn provides sustenance for mortals, but it is also the sacred food. It is greedy—you must never grow it in the same patch of ground two years running. And to make it grow, the gods have to be satisfied.

DANCES AND SPECTATORS

Shalako at the winter solstice is probably the most famous of the so-called Kachina dances that the Zuñi and their neighbors perform each year. *Kachinas* are spiritual beings who act as intermediaries between people and the Great Spirit and who also act as messengers between the pueblo and the Rain People. The Kachinas manifest themselves as clouds that bring rain to the arid fields. Shalako is held every December in the Zuñi pueblo to celebrate the end of the old year and the beginning of the new year, and to bless all of the houses of the pueblo that have been erected during the year. The dancers' costumes are splendors of vivid color and design: towering, grotesque figures some ten feet (three meters) or more high, the head is like a bird's and yet the body is conical and covered with feathers, paint, and animal skins. The ceremony begins at sundown with a ritual crossing of the small river that runs through the pueblo. Then the procession makes its way around all the streets. The dancers' giant masks represent the couriers of the rain deities as they come to bless new homes, and they take most of the night to complete the circuit before the new dawn breaks. Because the pueblo is at a high elevation—over 7,000 feet (2,100 meters) —the night is cold.

Although the public is excluded from many other tribes' ceremonial dances, the Zuñi believe that if they were to exclude outsiders the ceremonies would have no effect. The dances are a necessity in dealing with the otherworldly. Many spectators come from far and wide to watch, but the dances are not for them unless they are themselves part of the nation who have made the return pilgrimage home from the cities of the southwestern United States where many of them now live. Their roots lie only just below the surface.

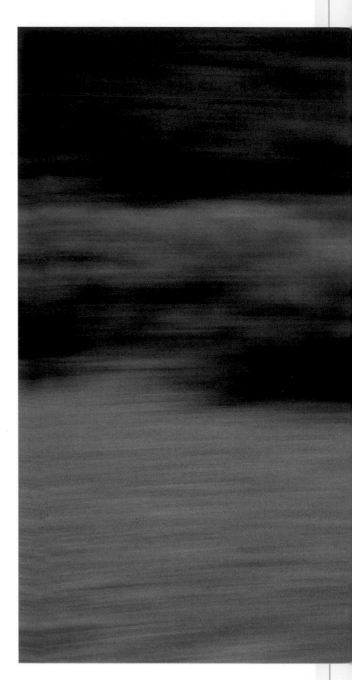

RIGHT: *The young men and boys taking part in the Corn Mountain relay races, held every midsummer, hope to ensure that the sun has the strength to continue on its return journey to a winter home.*

Deep in devotion. The continuing flow of pilgrims to the shrine of the Black Madonna of Czestochowa have helped preserve Poland as the most Catholic country in modern Europe.

JOURNEY FOUR

Czestochowa

ON EVERY CHURCH PORCH in Poland hangs a notice advertising a pilgrimage to Czestochowa to venerate the nation's patron, the Black Madonna. Large parishes organize their own pilgrimages; smaller parishes join a diocesan or a regional pilgrimage. The Pauline Church of the Holy Ghost in Warsaw has been the starting point for a great annual walking pilgrimage to Czestochowa since as long ago as 1711.

LEFT: *"Blessed art thou among women. . . ."*
Popular devotion to the Queen of Poland
remained strong through long years of rule
by outside forces, whether Swedish, imperial
Russian, Prussian, Nazi, or Soviet.

Pilgrims—a third of a million, the vast majority of them Poles—travel to Czestochowa in August for the Feast of the Assumption. Some go by train on "pilgrim specials" through the broad, flat, and featureless central region of Poland into the mountains of the south. On ill-made roads, buses and old Soviet-era cars mingle with German-manufactured faster and sleeker models, but there are still some that make the journey by horse and cart. They all converge on a gaunt industrial town overlooked by one of the nation's prime baroque church complexes to celebrate, not only Poland's national saint, but the Polish nation itself.

QUEEN OF POLAND

Our Lady of Czestochowa has a special place in the hearts of Poles. Her protection began over three hundred years ago. "The Deluge"—a translation of the Polish term *Potop*—was a devastating mid-seventeenth-century war between the Poles and first the Cossacks, then the Swedes. The Swedes swiftly occupied the whole of Poland in 1655. At first, the Poles put up little resistance; but in 1666, with the lifting of the Swedish siege of the monastery of Jasna Góra at Czestochowa, the tide turned in Polish favor. On April 1, 1656 Poland's elected king, Jan II Kazimierz (Jan Casimir), proclaimed Matka Boska, the Mother of God, to be "Queen of Poland," and special veneration of the image of the Virgin at Jasna Góra began—a veneration that lasts to this day.

The icon became the symbol of the unity and the liberty of the Catholic Poles, initially against the Protestant Swedes, and thereafter against successive occupiers of Poland and enemies of its religion—Prussians, Russians, Nazis, and Communists.

JASNA GÓRA

Enormous steel works and textile mills loom over the town of Czestochowa, one of the largest and most industrialized in the region. A mile (or few kilometers) away from the center of the city is the

LEFT: An air of holiday is never far away outside the monastery of Jasna Góra. The stern exterior and swirling baroque interior shelter the icon that is the most treasured possession of Poland.

monastery of Jasna Gora (Bright Peak.) It was founded for the Pauline order, the Monks of St. Paul of the Desert, in 1382 at the behest of the king, Ludwik Wigierski (Ludwig the Hungarian). There were soon pilgrims from all over eastern Europe—Poland, Prussia, Hungary, and Silesia—visiting the shrine of the Czarna Madonna (the Black Madonna). The Byzantine icon of the Virgin Mary and Christ Child probably came to Jasna Góra from what is now Ukraine in 1384—which was probably not long after it was painted.

Eastern Europe was wracked by religious controversy in the fifteenth century. In Holy Week, 1430, the sacred image was attacked by Hussites—followers of Jan Hus (or Huss) who were Reformation iconoclasts before their time. They tore the icon from its altar and took it into the forecourt, where they attacked it with swords. Finally the image was transfixed with a dagger. (Legend has it that the attackers were immediately struck down by divine retribution.) Over the course of the next few years, King Władysław II Jagieło commissioned workshops to repair the image. The broken panels were pieced together, a frame made for them, and a copy of the original painting created in tempera on canvas and stretched over the frame. The Virgin's head is covered with a dark cape edged in gold and spangled with fleurs-de-lis, and her eyes are half-closed and downcast, as if filled with tears. In the attack, two deep wounds were scratched in the left cheek of the face of the Virgin, and they remain as a memorial of that event—although legends say that however hard the restorers tried to erase the marks, they reappeared.

News of the almost miraculous restoration of the Virgin's portrait brought pilgrims to Czestochowa once more in the thousands. Some claimed miraculous cures, and the Pauline monastery became one of the most popular pilgrimage shrines in Europe. The church's tall and slender tower is still as much a defining element on the town's skyline as the industrial buildings have become. The Madonna is housed in a separate building on the north side of the monastery church, in the Chapel of the Nativity of the Virgin.

Great treasures were donated to the monastery and the Madonna, including the seventeenth-century high altar of ebony and silver, with silver screens in front, where the image has since been displayed. The icon has many sets of garments to "wear," all studded with jewels and sewn with precious metals, and there are thousands of gold and silver objects and sacred vessels in the monastery's treasury. Many artists contributed to the revived monastery's great swirling baroque Italianate plaster-and-paint decoration as it was transformed into a basilica befitting the shrine of the Queen of the Polish Crown, as she was proclaimed in 1717. Uniquely in Poland's troubled history, the treasure-house of Jasna Góra has survived unscathed despite being besieged by the Swedes in 1655 and by the Russians under Catherine II in 1770 and again in 1920, when the icon image is also said to have appeared in the sky. Some take that as a sign of divine protection.

BLACK MADONNAS

One of the characteristics of the Virgin and Child at Jasna Góra is that their skin is depicted as black, or at least very dark. Despite attempts to explain this phenomenon as the effects of centuries of candle smoke and tarnish, the fact remains that there are many Black Madonnas in Europe, and many of them are very ancient. In Einsiedeln in Switzerland, Mariazell in Austria, Chartres and Rocamadour in France, and Monserrat in Spain, similar figures are notable for their negritude. In a continent filled with white faces, the Black Madonnas possess an added air of mystery.

POLISH CATHOLICISM

Poland's tradition of religious toleration in the six-teenth century was transformed by Jesuit zeal into a fierce devotion to Roman Catholicism in the course of the seventeenth. The country was then invaded by Protestant Germany and Orthodox Russia, both of whom gained control of at least part of the once-sovereign nation, and in due course the notion that "to be a Pole is to be a Catholic" came to be a truism. A major part of the re-Catholicization of Poland was the emphasis placed upon veneration of the saints and, in particular, the Mother of God. The Czarna Madonna, and many other portraits and statues of the Virgin, became the centerpieces of elaborate observances.

During the long years of Communist rule after World War II, when there was an uneasy coexis-tence with the Catholic Church, pilgrimages wend-ing their way to Czestochowa from all over Poland became potent symbols of defiance. A band of stu-dents 25,000 strong would set out every year from Warsaw for the ten-day walk to Czestochowa, camping or sleeping rough, starting each day with Mass before setting off on the next leg, and avoid-ing the blandishments of the Communist-placed *agents provocateurs* who tried to subvert their faith.

BELOW: *Pilgrims come to Czestochowa from all over Poland, especially for the August Feast of the Assumption. Many of them will be exhausted at journey's end after their long approach on foot.*

Arriving on the Feast of the Assumption, they would take their place in the long line for their fleeting glimpse of the Madonna and to participate in the vast celebration of Mass. Today, distributing communion to a crowd approaching a million strong is no mean feat, but the pilgrims are secure in the knowledge that the monastery has been perfectly able to cope over the centuries.

The Czarna Madonna came to international attention in the 1970s. Cardinal Karol Wojtyła of Krakow was elected Pope in 1978, taking the title John Paul II. Returning to his native land the following year, he made sure that Czestochowa was prominent on his itinerary, and a third of the nation turned out to see the Pope on this tour. Within a few months the free trade-union movement, *Solidarnošč* (Solidarity) was born, under the leadership of Lech Wałesa, an electrician from the Gdansk shipyards. Strikes and demonstrations—and military repression—followed, not least in the industrial and mining region above which Jasna Góra stands. On the shipyard strikers' picket-line fences fluttered images of the Czarna Madonna.

Within ten years the Communist regime that Solidarity opposed had collapsed and Lech Wałesa himself became Poland's president—events leaving some with no doubt that the Czarna Madonna had saved Poland once more. The Catholic Church is discovering that it is losing some of its hold over the Polish population now that political goals have been realized, but few believe that the hold of the Czarna Madonna has diminished. Large numbers of pilgrims continue to come. Situated behind the movable screen that allows the faithful glimpses of the icon at prescribed times of the day, she still has a firm hold on the hearts of Poles.

RIGHT: The image of the Black Madonna and Child is to be found throughout Poland and wherever Polish communities have been established throughout the world.

During the celebrations each Pentecost of the Virgin Mary of El Rocío, traditional and modern-day aspects of Andalucia mingle together. Although the annual pilgrimage has remained a local devotion, it has also become a national media circus.

El Rocío

IF YOU READ *bumper stickers, you may well see one on the back of an Andalucian car in southwestern Spain that reads Soy Rociero ("I am a Rociero".) The driver will be really proud that he or she joined the throng for at least one of the annual pilgrimages that are a characteristic feature of this region of Iberia. About ten miles (sixteen kilometers) from a dead end in the coastal road in western Andalucia is a place so small that it might not even be on the map were it not for the romería or pilgrimage every Pentecost.*

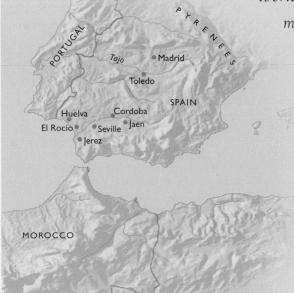

ABOVE: *Her crown shines out above a sea of her devotees as Our Lady is taken from the shrine and presented to the pilgrims who have made often long and arduous journeys to pay homage to her.*

El Rocío's is the biggest and possibly the oldest pilgrim procession in Spain. Hundreds of thousands of pilgrims come every year, arriving in horse-drawn covered wagons that are decked out in flowers and multicolored streamers. They camp in the fields, spend a few days making merry, and then return home again. Quintessentially Andalucian, revelry and religious devotion go hand in hand.

PAST AND PRESENT

This pilgrimage is unique not only in Andalucia but also in the whole of Spain. Indeed it is one of the amazing spectacles of the world. A mixture of the sacred, the profane, the bucolic, and the violent, perhaps it could only happen in this quarter of Spain, for Andalucia itself seems to embody all those attributes. Seville, the principal city of the region, is not far away, and the pious processions and religious carnival of *Santa Semana* (Holy Week) will have only four or five weeks previously been concluded with fireworks and street displays going up in flames. Some of the brotherhoods that take part in those demonstrations of piety then swiftly turn their thoughts to the journey to El Rocío.

The "modern" processions began back in the thirteenth century after a local shepherd discovered a statue of the Virgin Mary in a hollow tree. Deciding to take her home with him, he found that when he woke up after taking a nap on the way the statue had disappeared. It had gone back to the tree of its own accord. When the local villagers of Almonte tried to help him, the statue did the same again. It seemed clear that the statue did not wish to move, so a shrine was built on the spot, and healing miracles were soon reported there.

Pentecost—the late spring feast commemorating how Christ's apostles received the Holy Spirit shortly after Christ's Ascension to heaven—became the main occasion for pilgrimage. The hordes still converge on El Rocío at that time to venerate the Virgin, a white life-size statue with a gold crown. Wearing six stiff white petticoats, she is Nuestra Señora del Rocío, La Paloma Blanca (White Dove) —and the Queen of the Marshes. The shrine and village lie on the edge of the great Doñana National Park, 15,060 square miles (39,000 square kilometers) in extent and the largest in Europe, with its marshland bird and wildlife habitats.

The Church of the Virgin is a pink and white confection of the 1760s, replacing a sequence of older buildings. Yet worship and pilgrimage on this site undoubtedly goes back much further than the medieval origins that the legends record. Like Santiago de Compostela, this site is very close to the coastline, at the edge of the then-known world. Evidence of worship of a Venus-type goddess is recorded here from the Roman and Visigothic periods, and the mother goddess cult may well go back deep into unrecorded time.

BROTHERLY LOVE AND RIVALRY

Hermanidades (brotherhoods) from Huelva, Seville, and from towns and villages all over Andalucia converge on El Rocío to visit the shrine. These brotherhoods are first recorded almost four hundred years ago, although many (Triana, Umbrete, and Coria del Rio among them) were founded in the early nineteenth century and others still in the twentieth century during the 1910s and 1930s. The years just before the Spanish Civil War saw the biggest rush of foundations, as the battle for hearts and minds between a religious right and a socialist left in the country at large was translated into devotion in Andalucia. There were no pilgrimages during the principal war years themselves, 1937–38, but the pilgrimages were to flourish once more in the Franco years.

Each bearing its own simpecado, a miniature shrine to the Virgin of El Rocío, the decorated carts that traditionally accompany the pilgrims at Pentecost trundle along the Doñana marshland routes to the great shrine.

ABOVE: *Jostled by a press of humanity, many of the pilgrims have taken days to reach the shrine. The Virgin's statue is borne aloft and paraded round all the brotherhoods assembled in this tiny place. Hymns, bands, loudspeakers, and the shouts of the crowd all combine in a cacophony of sound and devotion.*

It takes a year's planning—and up to a week's traveling for those who come on horseback or in the covered wagons, some drawn by horses, others by oxen. Each wagon has its own mini-shrine, a *simpecado*, with a picture of the Virgin. They come from Seville and Huelva, Trigueros, Dos Hermanas, Jerez de la Frontera, Olivares, and throughout the region. Since the 1970s new pilgrim brotherhoods have journeyed from further afield; from Córdoba, Jaén, Toledo, and even the Canary Islands and Brussels. The brotherhood from the Andalucian hill town of Ronda travels from the Monday to the Thursday in the week before Pentecost, its wagons and carts forming an orderly procession governed by the "mayor of carts." Overnight they stay in La Corchuela, Playero, and Los Palacios, sleeping in their vehicles or under the stars.

Buses, cars, and four-wheel-drive off-road vehicles bring even greater numbers of pilgrims, many of them ferried across the Guadalquivir river by the obliging Spanish army. The pilgrimage has often enjoyed royal patronage—Queen Sofia of Spain has been among the pilgrims in recent years. The Pope himself came in 1993.

The pilgrimage is now such a huge phenomenon that it has become a logistical nightmare and a health hazard in waiting. The pilgrim scenes are broadcast live on television, and there are usually TV- or radio-documentary crews recording the events for their viewers or listeners in different parts of the world. The pilgrimage thereby becomes a virtual experience for those who cannot be there themselves.

SACRED AND PROFANE

The object of all this journeying may be deeply religious, but the experience en route may often be quite the opposite. Pilgrims wash down copious quantities of paella with huge drafts of wine. The sound from the ghetto blasters is more often the music of the streets than of the cloister. It is an occasion for license as well as reverence.

On the Saturday evening, when the pilgrims are finally assembled, each brotherhood files past the shrine to pay its respects to the Virgin. This colorful line of pilgrims, solemn and exuberant at the same time, dirty with dust and sweat from the road, is one of the moving and emotional aspects of the pilgrimage. Temporarily the emotions and excesses of the journey are forgotten in the collective ritual. An outdoor mass is said in the village square on the Pentecost Sunday morning, followed by bouts of drinking and dancing. Then on Monday morning, the senior brotherhood, the *Hermanidad de Almonte*, takes the Virgin from her shrine to visit all the little simpecados. She is greeted by cries, "¡Viva la Paloma Blanca!" "¡Guapa!" A pilgrim wishing to help carry the Virgin or even just touch the hem of her petticoats must fight for the honor. The *Almonteños* from the town of Almonte will attempt to repel the rowdy, and fists will fly, fueled by alcohol as well as religious zeal.

Some will recite the prayers of the shrine:

El Rocío is a collective olé *piercing the air of Andalucia, across valleys and hills, fields and mountains, rivers and marshes. It becomes a great* Salve Regina *(Hail, Holy Queen) placed at the feet of the White Dove as she shines forth from the white stones of her shrine. . . . El Rocío does not speak, does not describe, does not define. El Rocío intuits, feels, lives. But it does not define. . . . Oh Lord, El Rocío is heaven on earth.*

Eventually the Virgin has made her rounds and is returned to the shrine, awaiting her outing next Pentecost. The oxcarts, horses, buses, and cars leave the village, carrying away pilgrims who often nurse hefty hangovers as well as cleansed souls. El Rocío returns to its quiet slumbers once more.

A candlelight vigil at the shrine of Our Lady of Fátima. Devotion to the Mother of God is intense in Portugal, and many local as well as national shrines are dedicated to her.

JOURNEY SIX

Fátima and Lamego

THE ENGLISH LANGUAGE *has just one word—pilgrimage—to describe a specifically religious journey, whereas Portuguese, like Spanish, has a whole variety of words. A* romería, *for example, is a localized event: a pilgrimage to a shrine that may be no farther than the edge of a village or that is the point of focus for a small country area. A* peregrição *is a much wider event, of regional or national importance. In Portugal, religion is intertwined with everyday life, and the saints occupy a particular place in the affections of local communities throughout the country. More people regularly attend church than in almost any other European country, and the holidays are still predominantly holy days.*

Throughout the country, and especially in the northern half, pilgrimages and saints' feasts are all part of the year-round cycle of celebrations and events.

Votive statues of Our Lady and the shrines of saints are dotted around everywhere—at the sides of the roads, in little wayside chapels, in separate and grander chapels, and in the parish churches. The annual celebration at Lamego of Nossa Senhora dos Remédios (Our Lady of Cures) in September is a hybrid of the two, *romería* and *peregrição*, while the shrine of Our Lady of Fátima is of national—indeed, global—significance.

A TOWN'S FEAST: LAMEGO

Lying just south of the River Douro, Lamego is set among hills famous for the vineyards that make the wine for port. On top of the highest hill overlooking the town, at 2,000 feet (605 meters), stands the Church of Nossa Senhora dos Remédios. A monumental granite and whitewashed double flight of steps climbs the steep hillside to the church from the town's central avenue. The outdoor staircase is a baroque experience in its own right, with its traditional blue tiles (*azulejos*) depicting religious scenes. Urns decorate the balconies that are the regular stopping places. The stopping places are not just there to allow the visitor to admire the view, for this is also a penitential staircase. Some pilgrims to the shrine ascend on their knees, members of their family supporting them as they go. Whimpers of pain mingle with their prayers, especially from those pilgrims who have opted not to wear knee pads. On the procession day of September 8 and in the weeks around it, Lamego celebrates. Yet there are reminders everywhere that this shrine is to Our Lady of Cures—the limbless, the sick, and the dying ask for the alms and the prayer of others.

On the feast day itself, the statue of Our Lady is taken down the staircase and placed in a flower-filled cart that then follows the processional route. The town streets are packed with onlookers, while the best bedspreads are hung from the balconies of houses that overlook the route. Other carts carry tableaux from the life of the Virgin, in which local children take up the roles. One particularly lucky girl is chosen to be Mary at the Annunciation. Special papal dispensation is required for these carts to be drawn by oxen, humble beasts of burden—although these may well be the most coiffeured and preened oxen you are ever likely to see.

Following behind the procession are faces familiar from other parts of the festival: the woman who had crawled up the staircase shrieking in pain; the man whose wooden leg and withered arm were prominently displayed to help coax pilgrims and

BELOW: The figure of Our Lady at the Annunciation is drawn on an oxcart through the streets of Lamego on the annual feast day that attracts pilgrims from throughout nothern Portugal.

Descending the final stages of the penitential staircase with care and awe, an elderly pilgrim will soon arrive into the bustle of the town of Lamego on its big annual feast day.

passersby to give him a few coins; the elderly woman whose face lit up in the chapel when she was given her indulgence—the piece of paper promising time off in Purgatory—for having made the pilgrimage on the feast day.

Once the procession is over and night falls, the fireworks start. A huge display of alarmingly home-made rockets fills the sky. And as Our Lady of Cures goes back into her shrine for another year, a night's drinking and feasting begins.

THE SECRETS OF FÁTIMA

It is barely 150 miles (240 kilometers) from Lamego to Fátima. The pilgrimages to Fátima are mostly of more recent origin than those to Lamego or the *romerías* to countless local shrines throughout Portugal. Yet Fátima has a significance for the nation and the Catholic world well beyond the reach of those local celebrations.

On May 13, 1981, Pope John Paul II was shot in front of a vast crowd in St. Peter's Square, Rome. The attempted assassination failed, but the Pope was seriously wounded. As he fell, he later recalled, the word "Madonna" was on his lips. And in his mind was the image of Jesus' mother—in particular, Our Lady of Fátima. And in the modern and highly politicized world, prophetic visions that occurred in 1917 to three poor shepherd children in northern Portugal still reverberate.

Three *pastorinhos* (shepherd children) saw the Virgin Mary appear to them six times, the first on May 13 and the last on October 13, 1917, in a holm oak tree at Cova da Iria near the small town of Fátima. The cousins Lúcia dos Santos, Francisco Marta, and Jacinta Marta, age ten, nine, and seven

LEFT: Their candles lighting up the darkness, pilgrims have made their way from all over Portugal and beyond to share in the devotions commemorating Our Lady's appearances since 1917.

respectively, received the visions, and the eldest child was able to converse with Our Lady. They were given three secrets, as well as the information that only one of them would survive for much longer. At the time of the last vision, no fewer than seventy thousand people came to witness the event, and—skeptic and believer alike—were presented with what immediately became known as the Miracle of the Sun. The sun seemed to dance in the sky and then zigzagged toward the ground, while an unearthly light filled the heavens. Some blind people claimed the light had healed them.

One prediction came true. The two younger children were soon to be victims of the influenza epidemic that was then ravaging the world. They lie buried in the basilica built to honor the visions

ABOVE: The strength of continuing devotion at Fátima is clear in this photograph taken in 1949, with pilgrims kneeling in the stony fields, and at the modern basilica subsequently erected on the site (right).

(and were beatified in 1989). Only Lucía survived, becoming a Carmelite nun in Coimbra, where she lives to this day.

What were the visions of these three children? In 1941 Sister Lucía dos Santos divulged the secrets of Fátima to her bishop, including a third secret that was to remain undisclosed for a further fifty-nine years. As Sister Lucía told him:

The first part is the vision of hell. Our Lady showed us a great sea of fire which seemed to be under the earth. Plunged in this fire were demons and souls in human form, like transparent burning embers, all

*This elderly present-day pilgrim kneels penitentially on the
hard ground as she approaches the site where three pastorinhos
saw the Virgin Mary in a sequence of six visions.*

blackened or burnished bronze, floating about in the conflagration . . . and amid shrieks and groans of pain and despair, which horrified us and made us tremble with fear.

We then looked up at Our Lady, who said to us so kindly and so sadly, . . . "The war [World War I] is going to end – but if people do not cease offending God, a worse one will break out during the Pontificate of Pius XI. When you see a night illumined by an unknown light, know that this is the great sign given you by God that he is about to punish the world for its crimes, by means of war, famine and persecutions of the Church and of the Holy Father. To prevent this, I shall come to ask for the consecration of Russia to my Immaculate Heart. . . ."

The vision offered the children a portent of hell and a prediction of what has usually been taken to be World War II and the conquering atheism of the Soviet Union.

Finally, in the summer of 2000, once the process of dismantling the former Communist states of Eastern Europe was well advanced, the third secret was finally revealed—a secret that at least two popes had previously read and deemed unsuitable for publication. Sister Lucía recalled the vision in her testimony, originally dictated in 1941:

And we saw in an immense light that is God—something similar to how people appear in a mirror when they pass in front of it—a bishop dressed in white. We had the impression that it was the Holy Father. Other bishops, priests, men and women religious were going up a steep mountain, at the top of which there was a big cross of rough-hewn trunks like a cork tree with the bark on. Before reaching it the Holy Father passed through a big city half in ruins and, trembling with halting step, afflicted with pain and sorrow, he prayed for the souls of the corpses he met on his way. Having reached the top of the mountain, on his knees at the foot of the big cross, he was killed by a group of soldiers who fired bullets and arrows at him, and in the same way there died one after another the other bishops, priests, men and women religious, and various lay people of different ranks and positions. Beneath the two arms of the cross there were two angels each with a crystal aspersorium in one hand in which they gathered up the blood of the martyrs and with it sprinkled the souls that were making their way to God.

The apocalyptic vision seemed to predict the assassination of the pope, or at least an attempt on the pope's life like that of 1981. It was little wonder, then, that successive pontiffs had found the secret so startling. Although many Fátima-watchers were disappointed with the third secret, having been hoping at the very least for the date of the end of the world, it was still shocking.

A NATION'S SHRINE

After the assassination attempt of May 13, 1981, it appeared evident to Pope John Paul II that it was "a mother's hand that guided the bullet's path," enabling him to halt "at the threshold of death." And when the Bishop of Leiria-Fátima visited Rome afterward, the Pope gave him the bullet, which had lodged in his jeep after the assassination attempt, so that it might be kept in the shrine. The bullet was actually set in the crown of the statue of Our Lady of Fátima.

Our Lady of Fátima became a central plank in Portugal's image of itself in the twentieth century. She appeared, inconveniently for the authorities, during a time when the Portuguese government was fiercely anticlerical and feared the outpouring of popular religious emotion. During the long years of Fascist dictatorship between 1926 and 1974, under António de Oliveira Salazar and his successors, she became the supreme symbol of the state. Portugal, however, was kept in the straitjacket of the past. Our Lady of Fátima was nonetheless made patroness of Portugal, and the shrine—"the altar of Portugal"—has been the biggest pilgrimage site in the nation ever since those huge crowds witnessed the Miracle of the Sun.

A vast, and ugly, basilica church was consecrated in 1953. (Even the Church authorities now admit that it lacks architectural good taste.) An esplanade in front overlooks the smaller chapel and accommodates half a million pilgrims—the majority of them Portuguese—on May 13 or October 13. Glass doors protect the site of the visions. The candles at the shrine are 6 feet (1.8 metres) or more. One particular tradition of the celebrations is the procession for High Mass, when the Virgin's statue is carried aloft to the basilica and the pilgrims wave their white handkerchiefs at her. Elsewhere, the commercialism is intense, as plastic and plaster images of the Virgin compete with each other in ever more lurid colors. Miracles have been claimed, although none have been verified—but that does not deter the devout. On the main days of pilgrimage, as many as twenty or thirty thousand people make the pilgrimage to the shrine on foot, some in penitentially bare feet, through the often inhospitable countryside.

Since the army-led "Carnation Revolution" of 1974, when the old dictatorship was overthrown, Portugal has changed dramatically. The power of the Church has been reduced, yet the hold of the pilgrim sites remains strong. Sacred and profane often happily combine. Holy days and holy places are part of the very fabric of Portuguese society.

BELOW: The thickets of candles are the symbol of the prayers that the faithful at Fátima send heavenward. Pope John Paul II's own devotion to Our Lady of Fátima has given her shrine a renewed confidence.

The headdress and costume of this dancer outside Mexico's national shrine to the Virgin of Guadalupe combine Aztec elements with the Catholicism that was brought from Spain.

JOURNEY SEVEN

Guadalupe

A MIXTURE OF PROUD PATRIOTISM and intense piety, the journey to venerate Mexico's national treasure, the Virgin of Guadalupe, is one of the most intense religious experiences of central America. Devotion to Our Lady has been one of the most important elements in the development of a specifically Mexican tradition of spirituality for nearly five centuries and is one of the defining forces in modern Mexican society. The image of the dark Virgin— la Virgen Morena—permeates life throughout Mexico and beyond, especially in Hispanic areas of the United States and Canada. Now Hispanic and Native American cultures combine in this popular cult of the Virgin, and the scale of the pilgrimage to her shrine is overshadowed only by a few other great Christian sites.

TEXAS

MEXICO

Durango

Guadaiajara

Guadalupe
Mexico City

Acapulco

YUCATAN
PENINSULA

GUATEMALA

In 1519, the Spaniard Hernan Cortes arrived in the capital of Mexico, Tenochtitlan, to parley with the Mexican emperor Moctezuma. Within two years, the Spaniards had overthrown the imperial civilization and established themselves as rulers of New Spain. Cortes set about dismantling the old capital and building a new settlement, Mexico City, in its place. By 1531, only the Maya of southern Mexico and Guatemala remained unconquered. Yet in that year—according to legend—an event occurred that would shape a new nation.

THE LEGEND OF TEPEYAC

In 1531, the Virgin Mary—Our Lady with a dark complexion—suddenly appeared to a man named Juan Diego, a native Nahua and a person of no particular rank or status. As a recent convert, Diego was on his way to Mass when he heard a sweet voice calling him affectionately. It happened at a place called Tepeyacac, later known as Tepeyac, then Guadalupe, just north of Mexico City. The apparition sent Juan Diego to the bishop-elect of Mexico, Juan de Zumárraga, with instructions to have a church built in her honor—a common request of the Virgin whenever she makes a visionary appearance. Although the bishop was skeptical, he insisted that Juan Diego go back and ask for a sign of confirmation. He did, and the Virgin told Diego to go to a hill, where he found

BELOW: Some of the millions of pilgrims to the basilica of the Virgin of Guadalupe perform costumed plays and traditonal dances in the square outside, adding to the color and spectacle.

The miraculous image of the Virgin of Guadalupe, divinely
imprinted on Juan Diego's cloak, hangs above the national flag
in the great basilica on the outskirts of Mexico City.

In the vast new basilica dedicated to the Virgin of Guadalupe, all eyes are fixed on the wondrous image. This is one of the most-visited Christian pilgrimage sites in the world.

roses blooming out of season. Gathering them up in his cloak, he returned to the bishop, and let them fall to the floor. On the cloak a miraculous picture of the Virgin had left its imprint and de Zumárraga ordered that a chapel be built at once.

Although the story is widely known, there are no reliable documentary sources that date before the mid-seventeenth century. The first reference to a shrine at Tepeyac dates only from the 1550s, and the first firm evidence for the painting dates from 1606. There are therefore awkward historical gaps in the accounts of events.

THE BIRTH OF MEXICO

Regardless, if not in 1531, Mexico may have been born in 1648, when the legend was first published in Mexico City—a legend that was European in form but featured a Native American, the Nahua Juan Diego, as the main human figure. First published in Spanish, it was translated the following year into Nahuatl, the native language, by Luis Laso de la Vega in a book usually known either under its short title *Huei tlamamhuiçoltica* or as *Nican mophua*. The dual publication was significant because the texts were designed to appeal to two different constituencies: the Native Americans and the Spanish-speaking but Mexican-born *Criollos* (Creoles). The effect on the native population was as yet indiscernible, but the effect on the Mexican-born Spanish was immediate and strong. These Criollos were people who saw themselves as marginalized and treated as inferior by the colonial administrators and clerics who came from Spain. Now beginning to call themselves *Americanos*, the Criollos had a strong group identity, the central icon of which was the Virgin of Tepeyac—known from the 1550s as the "Virgin of Guadalupe" after the royal monastery in central Spain with its own miraculous image of the Virgin and Child. Whether

her story was actually a contemporary invention or the embodiment of a century-old tradition, it was the catalyst the Criollos needed to begin on the road toward determining their own destiny, bringing in the native Mexican and *mestizo* population behind them. In the end, the legend became the most powerful tool that the nationalists were to possess.

MEXICAN NATIONALISM

From the 1650s, devotion to the Virgin of Guadalupe spread rapidly, throughout Mexico and into Spanish America. Although she appeared to a humble Nahua, it was felt she had really come as a sign of divine favor on Mexico itself. The notion of a specifically Mexican vision took such a hold that a century later Pope Benedict XIV would remark, quoting Psalm 147, "He has not done the like for any other nation." At the time, the movement was still not Indian but rather restricted largely to the newly emerging Americanos. Poor Juan Diego was hardly mentioned. Not until the eighteenth century did the legend begin to take hold among the native population, as preachers emphasized the need for devotion to the Virgin.

Then the Virgin of Guadalupe became a Mexican nationalist symbol. Mexico, people said, was born at Tepeyac. The sacred image was carried on the banners in Manuel Hidalgo's revolution of 1810. The troops vowed long life to her—and death to Spaniards. What followed became a war of the rival Virgins, since the royalists and Spaniards adopted *la Virgen dos Remédios*, otherwise known as *La Conquistadora*, as their symbol. Royalist troops even "executed" an effigy of the Guadalupe saint by firing squad. After Mexico gained its independence from Spain in 1821, the new state adopted the Virgin of Guadalupe as the national symbol of liberation. Then, in 1895, with papal blessing, the miraculous image was crowned.

ABOVE: Our Lady of the camper van. Given the road-traffic accident rates, Mexico's notorious drivers probably do need all the intervention and divine protection that heaven can provide.

Even then, the native Mexicans played only a minimal role in the proceedings. There is no evidence for the mass conversion of Mexicans after the establishment of the shrine, and the cult within the native population began in the eighteenth century. And it was not until the twentieth century that indigenous Mexicans' attachment to the Virgin of Guadalupe overtook that of the Hispanic people.

MIRACLES

Miracles were first attached to the shrine in the seventeenth century, when it was invoked against the great floods of 1629. The painting was taken to Mexico City where, so it was reported, it helped turn back the waters. Called upon again in the epidemic that ravaged Mexico in 1736 and 1737, the Virgin of Guadalupe "succeeded" where other sacred images had failed in stemming the tide of infection. Still, the Roman Catholic Church was slow to recognize the cult of Guadalupe. A feast-day was instituted in 1754, and following the papal permission for the coronation in 1895, the Virgin was proclaimed patroness of all Latin America in 1910. In 1945 she was dubbed Queen of Mexico and Empress of the Americas. Hedging his bets with the opening caveat "According to tradition," Pope Pius XII declared that brushes "not from here below left a most precious image painted on the mantle of poor Juan Diego." Finally, Juan Diego himself, the Nahua who had received the vision, was beatified in 1990.

SHRINE AND MANTLE

To get to the Virgin's shrine, the nearest metro station is called, appropriately, Basilica, only some three miles (six kilometers) north of the center of Mexico City. The old basilica of Guadalupe, La Colegiata, was begun in 1695 and completed in 1709. Endlessly expanded yet still too small to cope with the volume of pilgrims, the modern basilica was consecrated in 1976. The vast shrine consists of an enclosed atrium encompassing 55,000 square yards (46,000 square meters), facing no fewer than six churches alongside the great basilica itself. With some twenty million pilgrims and visitors a year it is the most visited Christian church in the world after St. Peter's in Rome. Although pilgrims come from far and wide—the Virgin of Guadalupe is, after all, Empress of the Americas—devotion to her is particularly intense in Mexico, and Mexicans make up the majority of visitors to the shrine. Devotion knows no bounds of age or sex, and Mexicans' gardens also often contain a homemade shrine, but nothing compares with the experience of visiting the real thing.

The approach to the basilica is made on foot. Many penitents make their way up the processional route on their knees, perhaps keening their own private songs and hymns, overtaken by loud, banner-waving, chanting, and drumming processions. Some visitors hope for a miraculous cure from an illness; most wish to exhibit their piety and wonder at their nation's greatest treasure. The church itself can accommodate ten thousand pilgrims at a time: a moving platform carries them past the painting, giving pilgrims enough time to see, but no time to dawdle.

The object they have all come to venerate has so far escaped the attempts of doubters to prove a worldly origin. The painting shows a brown-skinned woman who is surrounded by the sun and cloaked in a blue mantle covered with stars. She stands, hands clasped in prayer or in offering, on a crescent moon held up by an angel. The woman looks down, her head tilted to the right, with an expression of compassion and strength in her green eyes. She is almost certainly pregnant. The fabric on which the painting appears is coarse, yet the image is strong, the lines are sure, and the colors bright and clear. Human hands have clearly worked on some parts of the image, in some cases to add elements, in other cases to make the woman more Native American in appearance—but other parts, the central image in particular, continue to defy rational scientific analysis. Modern studies have also revealed that the eyes of the image contain tiny images of people, who some have identified as Juan Diego and the bishop-elect Juan de Zumárraga.

Whatever the truth, if the Virgin of Guadalupe is a "fake," then, like the Shroud of Turin, it defies the attempts of modern science to explain how it was created, given the techniques and artistry available either four hundred years ago or even today.

MEXICO'S VIRGIN

No visitor to the shrine at Tepeyac can fail to be impressed by the intensity of devotion to the Virgin of Guadalupe—their Virgin, Mexico's Virgin. Hispanic and Native American cultures combine in the ever-popular cult. The great day for celebration is December 12, the Virgin's feast. The night before, Native American dance groups whirl and turn in front of the basilica, and Mexicans light fires throughout the country. The notion of special election for the Mexican people is at odds with the realities of Mexican life and politics. Local writer Octavio Paz was eventually to lament, "The Mexican people, after more than two centuries of attempts and defeats, have faith only in the Virgin of Guadalupe and the National Lottery."

Praying at the Dome of the Rock on Eid al-Fitr, the last day of fasting during the Muslim month of Ramadan. Like many sites in Jerusalem, this is a holy place for Jews and Christians.

Jerusalem

MOST OF THE WORLD'S shrines and holy places attract pilgrims from particular religions and specific areas. Jerusalem, by contrast, draws people from a wide variety of nations and different cultural traditions. It is the place the three great Religions of the Book all have in common. At times, especially during the major religious festivals, those traditions meet head-on and clash. One brand of Christianity quarrels with another. Israeli Jew is set against Muslim Arab. Orthodox Jews reject the accommodation of the Liberals. The tensions are palpable.

LEFT: *A light to greet the Light of the World. The flame signifying the Resurrection of Christ is passed from one candle to another on the night before Easter in the Church of the Holy Sepulcher.*

What is remarkable about Jerusalem is that for well over a millennium, despite expulsions, wars, crusades, disputes, and doctrinal opposition, pilgrims have often coexisted and the city has survived.

CENTER OF THE WORLD

Although by convention maps indicate north at the top, or provide a symbol to tell us in which direction north lies, we speak about "orienting" ourselves. Facing the Orient, facing east, is to face Jerusalem. Indeed the thirteenth-century *Mappa Mundi*, housed at Hereford Cathedral, depicts the world, not with north as its axis, but with Jerusalem at its very center. Jerusalem has been the holy city at the heart of the Christian, Jewish, and Muslim traditions throughout the ages. Christians revere it as the site where Christ was crucified and rose again and where his followers had established the early Church. Jews, on the other hand, flocked to the city's great Temple (before the Romans destroyed it in AD 70) which housed the Ark of the Covenant—the physical evidence of the Chosen People's pact with God. And Muslims venerate Jerusalem because it was from the rock on the mount where that very temple stood that angels bore Muhammad (Mohammed) to heaven before returning him to earth.

Jerusalem does not have a closely prescribed routine of the sort that operates in, say, Mecca, or is associated with the long-sanctified round of the principal churches and saints' tombs of Rome. Jerusalem's pilgrims go to different places at differ-

BELOW: The panorama of the holy but divided city of Jerusalem, enclosed within the ancient walls. The gold dome of the mosque built on the Jewish Temple Mount is clearly visible to the left.

ent times, where they engage in very different forms of worship. The result is a continuous crossing and diverging of bodies, voices, and religious artifacts, as well as clashes between the different traditions and beliefs.

Jerusalem is not one holy city but a multitude of holy cities within a single physical space, all operating at the same time. Every pilgrim tradition brings its own view of the holy city—and a pilgrimage to Jerusalem usually reinforces that view however many contrary visions arise.

DIFFERING TRADITIONS

For Christians, what Jerusalem and the Holy Land around the city offer is the chance to meditate on places and moments that are central to their sense of themselves as religious believers. The garden where Jesus spent his last night, the route that

Jesus walked carrying his cross, the place of his Crucifixion and the Church of the Holy Sepulcher where he was buried, and the sites where he spoke to the masses or performed miracles are therefore all holy places to be visited during the course of a true pilgrimage. To tread where Jesus once walked has always been an essential part of Christian visits to Jerusalem.

Doctrinal differences help determine how different groups of pilgrims operate. In the Orthodox Christian tradition, following which the walls and screens of churches are crowded with images of Christ, his Holy Mother, and the saints, worshippers stand among them all "as if placed in paradise." An icon is a window into the sublime. Entering holy space, especially for the elderly who constitute the majority of Orthodox pilgrims, is a foretaste of their entry into eternity when they die. In the Latin (Western) tradition, knowledge of the

sacred is mobilized back toward activity in the world at large. Believers with their faith in the power of God are given models for behavior in accordance with that power. Religious art is educative rather than all-embracing, and the lessons of the scriptures are considered to be inspirational: they are meant to provoke an individual into action. In the Protestant tradition, Holy Writ—religious text and the words of the Bible in particular—is primary in importance. Hence the holy places other Christans venerate in Jerusalem are often distinct from those of Protestants, who place greater emphasis on personal contemplation and readings than on formal worship and on "checking off" the list of places to be visited.

ABOVE: The banks of candles burn continually in the Church of the Holy Sepulcher, the site of Christ's Crucifixion and burial, as present-day Christian pilgrims add their prayers and intentions to the millions of prayers and hopes that have preceded them.

GREEK ORTHODOX PILGRIMS

Traditionally, pilgrims from the Greek tradition come to the Holy Land in old age. They are preparing themselves for a good death and for being received into paradise. At some point in their pilgrimage they will be rebaptized in the River Jordan, wearing white funeral shrouds that they have bought in Jerusalem and will keep to be clothed in at their burial. What counts is their presence in Jerusalem at the holy feasts.

Treading in Christ's footsteps. Christian pilgrims carry palm branches and sing hosannas as they walk in the traditional procession on Palm Sunday, the beginning of Holy Week.

During Holy Week itself, which commemorates Christ's passion, death, and Resurrection, and at the Feasts of the Assumption of the Virgin and of the Exaltation of the Cross, Jerusalem is filled with elderly Greek pilgrims. (Fortunately for the infrastructure and the catering capacity of the city, the Orthodox adherence to older calendars means that these feasts are observed on different dates from the Latin tradition.) The high moment for all the Greek Orthodox participants is the Ceremony of the Holy Fire where they wait in darkness, jammed together into the Church of the Holy Sepulcher, above Christ's tomb, for the moment of Resurrection. Burning candles pass from hand to hand, the church is filled with flickering candlelight, and the pilgrims sing the *Christos Anesti*:

> *Christ is risen from the dead,*
> *by death trampling upon death,*
> *and to those in the tombs bestowing life.*

CATHOLIC PILGRIMS

Pilgrims from the old Roman tradition are not such sticklers for the liturgical calendar, and the theme of universal experience is less important to them. The largest proportion of Catholics come as organized groups from all over the world. They come to be renewed in their faith, by walking where Jesus walked and to come closer to God by following the gospel stories *in situ*. At times the pilgrims' prayers at the sites provide striking juxtapositions. Rosaries are said in the mosque built over the place from which Jesus is supposed to have ascended into heaven; or Catholic, Greek Orthodox, and Protestant pilgrims dodge each other on the Via Dolorosa, the route—according to tradition—through the old city Jesus took on his way to the cross and which almost all Christian pilgrims follow today.

Pilgrims at the end of that route crowd in both awe and high spirits into the Church of the Holy Sepulcher, where the oddities of Christian pilgrimage to Jerusalem become most pronounced. At least part of the fabric dates back to its construction by the Holy Roman Emperor Constantine in 325. Virtually the whole of non-Protestant Christendom is represented within the church—and even on top of it, for that is where the Ethiopian monks are based, in stone huts on the flat roofs, squeezed out from the main body of the church by all the other denominations. Under the so-called Status Quo of 1852, an Ottoman decree that still holds sway, the fierce disputes between Christian creeds were resolved. Custody was divided among Armenians, Greeks, Roman Catholics, Ethiopians, Syrians, and the Copts. Some areas within the church are administered communally, others by clergy from one denomination or another. The site of Golgotha, the place of Crucifixion, is divided between Greek Orthodox and Roman Catholic; and Christ's tomb, between those two Churches together with the Armenian and Coptic Churches. The Syrians only maintain a chapel at the back of the rotunda. The key to this precious church is held by a Muslim, who ceremonially unlocks it every morning.

PROTESTANT PILGRIMS

By contrast, Protestant pilgrimages to Jerusalem and the Holy Land tend to shy away from the traditional sites revered by Orthodox and Catholic Christians. Pilgrimage with its system of indulgences—offering time off in Purgatory before gaining entry to heaven—was one of the aspects of Catholicism that led to the sixteenth-century split from Rome. Pilgrimage became instead a metaphor for the path of life, as in John Bunyan's 1678 allegory *The Pilgrim's Progress*. Only in the mid-nineteenth century did pilgrimage to the Holy Land enter the Protestant tradition, aided in no small part by the organized tours led by Thomas Cook and the opening of the Suez Canal.

The holy city and the Holy Land are inspiring, but the real inspiration tends to be a one-to-one experience of God, not mediated through the big church buildings that represent almost two thousand years of Catholic and Orthodox piety. One of the principal focuses for Protestant pilgrims is the Garden Tomb, claimed (on what many now admit was shaky evidence) to be the true site of Christ's tomb in a small enclosure outside the Old City's walls. Some fundamentalist Protestants come because they are actively seeking the full reestablishment of Jerusalem as a Jewish city, preparing for God's true and Final Judgment.

BELOW: Jewish pilgrims at the Western Wall wear the tallit *(prayer shawl) and bear spears of plants—olive, pine, myrtle, and palm—at the traditional Feast of Tabernacles, Succoth.*

JEWISH PILGRIMAGE

Pilgrimage into Jerusalem from throughout Israel and Palestine was an ancient tradition of Judaism. Three times a year people would travel, sometimes long distances, from their home towns and villages to observe the great feasts: Passover, the Feast of Weeks, and the Feast of Tabernacles. (Later, Hanukkah, the Festival of Light, was added to this scheme to make a fourth pilgrimage event.) At Succoth, the Feast of Tabernacles, for example, the Jews followed the instructions given by God in Leviticus, to:

> *dwell in booths . . . that your generations may know that I made the people of Israel dwell in booths when I brought them out of the land of Egypt.*

The Hebrew word for these pilgrimage feasts is *hag* (clearly related to the Muslim *hajj*), and it implies moving in a circle and dancing, which were themselves among the principal activities associated with Jewish pilgrimage.

ABOVE: *The Western or Wailing Wall is all that remains of the Jewish Temple that was destroyed in AD 70. Soaring above it is the Dome of the Rock, the mosque built some six hundred years later which is itself one of the holiest sites of Islam.*

Pilgrimage was one of the acts of the true believer, and the repository of truth was the Ark of the Covenant in the Temple built by Solomon, son of David, at Jerusalem—the Ark that had been carried through the desert by the nomadic early Jews before it came to rest in Jerusalem. The Jews were dispersed after Titus destroyed the (rebuilt) Temple in AD 70. More than eighteen centuries were to pass before the Jews were able to regain their base in the Holy Land with the promise and finally the estab-lishment of the state of Israel. Longing for the opportunity to go on pilgrimage to Jerusalem had for all this time been a central aspect of Judaism; "Next year in Jerusalem" was, and continues to be, the Passover invocation throughout the long years of Diaspora when only a few Jews were permitted access to the holy sites.

Jewish settlement in and around Jerusalem started again in the nineteenth century, when Jerusalem was reopened to many different influences. With the establishment of the state of Israel in 1947, and then the Israeli capture of the previously divided city of Jerusalem in the Six Days' War of 1967, the city of Jerusalem has become Jewish once more. The fabric of the pre-Diaspora city is jealously preserved as holy for all the different traditions of Judaism.

The Temple that Christ knew was the Third Temple, built by Herod the Great and subsequently destroyed by Titus. What is now believed to have been part of its western wall is the Wailing Wall, where to this day Jews stand and express their grief at their loss and exile, pressing prayers written on pieces of paper into cracks between the wall's stones. Not only did they lose the Temple site to the Romans, but they subsequently lost it to the Muslims, third of the great monotheistic religions to emerge from the Middle East.

MUSLIM PILGRIMAGE

The beautiful gold-sheathed Dome of the Rock, built on top of the Temple Mount in the late seventh century, incorporates Islam's sense of continuity with Judaism—and also emphasizes the Jews' disinheritance from their traditional center. This was the site where, according to tradition, Abraham was ordered to sacrifice his son before divine intervention saved him. Its circular and octagonal form echoes the Christians' principal

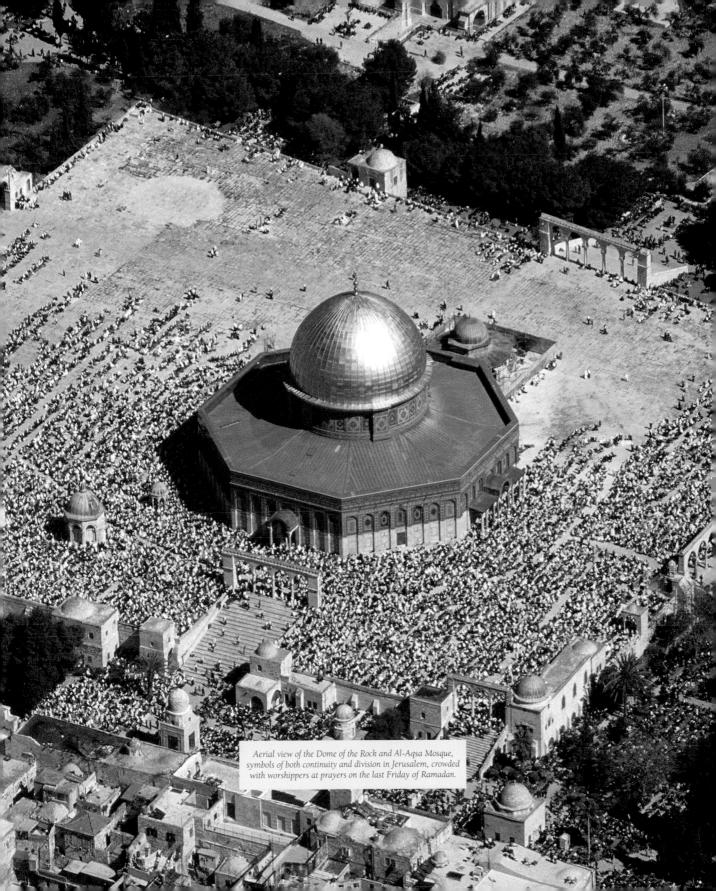

Aerial view of the Dome of the Rock and Al-Aqsa Mosque, symbols of both continuity and division in Jerusalem, crowded with worshippers at prayers on the last Friday of Ramadan.

shrine, the Holy Sepulcher. Yet this great mosque was erected here to commemorate the place from which Muhammad was taken to heaven by angels and then brought safely back to earth, making it a Muslim holy place almost to rival Mecca in the pilgrims it attracts and the wealth it has been given over the centuries. After Jerusalem was captured by Israel in the Six Days' War, the Dome of the Rock remained the symbol of the long centuries of Muslim control of the city and—since at times of political difficulty access is denied to pilgrims—as a focus for Arab Palestinian discontent.

ROOTED IN THE PAST

Pilgrimage was not an activity that Jesus instructed his followers to undertake; but, for the faithful, the urge to see the places mentioned in both the Old and the New Testaments was strong, even from Christianity's earliest days. When the Emperor Constantine established Christianity as the imperial religion in 313, Christians were given the ready opportunity to visit Jerusalem, as many did from the fourth century onward.

Palestine was wracked by conflict and invasion, so pilgrimage was a dangerous and lengthy activity whether by land or by sea. The Holy Sepulcher itself was burned by the Persians in 614, Muslim forces entered Jerusalem in 638, and the Holy Sepulcher was finally destroyed by the Muslim caliph in 1009. Although Jerusalem's Muslim rulers tolerated Christians' visiting the holy places, within strict limits, and the Byzantine emperor was permitted to rebuild part of the Sepulcher church in 1048, everything changed with the Crusades. Pope Urban II's militant call in 1095 to wrest the holy places from the grip of Islam resulted in the short-lived success of the First Crusade, when Jerusalem was retaken with hideous bloodshed in 1099 and the Christian Kingdom of Jerusalem was estab-

lished. To go on crusade was itself a pilgrimage, and the religious orders of knights—the Templars and the Hospitalers—were warrior pilgrims. Great crusader strongholds such as the castle of Krak des Chevaliers (Qalat al Hosn, Syria) guarded the pilgrims' and the soldiers' routes to Jerusalem, and the Church of the Holy Sepulcher was rebuilt, giving it more or less its present form and appearance.

Saladin reconquered Jerusalem for Islam in 1187, and the city remained under Muslim rule until the twentieth century. Christian pilgrimage continued, although the hardships were as great as ever. Medieval pilgrim ships regularly made the stormy voyage from Venice to Jaffa (Haifa). One pilgrim in 1413 was an English woman, Margery Kempe. Writing in the third person, she recalled:

> she thanked God with all her heart, praying him for his mercy that, just as he had brought her to see this earthly city of Jerusalem, he would grant her grace to see the blissful city of Jerusalem above, the city of heaven.

Other medieval pilgrimage centers prospered, preeminently Rome and Santiago de Compostela, as active Christian pilgrimage to the holy city of Jerusalem withered. In the nineteenth century, when the cult of the Orient and the systematic study of archaeology came into vogue, travelers rediscovered the mystery and appeal of Jerusalem. The ultimate success of Zionism, the cause for the reestablishment of a Jewish territorial homeland, brought the Jews back into Jerusalem's own particular melting pot and into direct conflict with their Arab Muslim counterparts.

The bustle, the tension, the unending disputes, commercialism, and antagonistic pieties would appear to detract from the appeal of Jerusalem. Yet these are exactly the aspects that give the city its vibrancy and its edge. Time, creed, and place are constantly overlapping in the earthly city that still for many pilgrims presages the blissful city above.

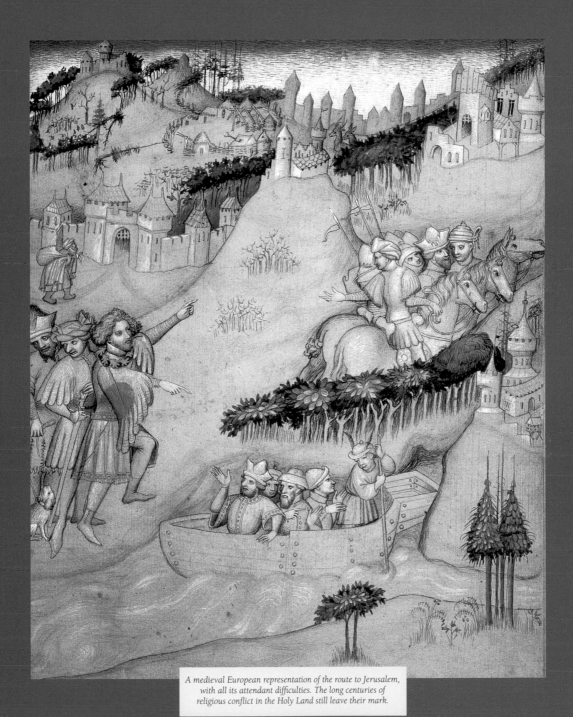

*A medieval European representation of the route to Jerusalem,
with all its attendant difficulties. The long centuries of
religious conflict in the Holy Land still leave their mark.*

Dawn breaks at Adam's Peak, one of two sites in southern Sri Lanka that is sacred to Buddhists, Hindus, Muslims, and Christians. Ascending the peak and following the ritual circuit at nearby Kataragama both confer deep spiritual grace.

JOURNEY NINE

Kataragama and Adam's Peak

ON THE ISLAND OF SERENDIPITY, known today as Sri Lanka, the two sacred sites of Kataragama and Adam's Peak are common to several religions. Hindu, Buddhist, Muslim, Christian, and indigenous native forms of worship are carried out side by side.

WESTERN GHATS

INDIA

Mangalore

Bangalore

Mysore

Madras

KERALA

Madurai

Jaffna

SRI LANKA

Colombo

Kandy

Adam's Peak

Kataragama

RIGHT: A spearhead through a Tamil woman's cheek indicates she has made a personal vow at Kataragama that she fervently intends to keep.

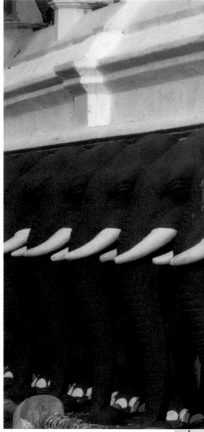

ABOVE: A band of Hindu pilgrims—the minority population in modern Sri Lanka—from the north of the island seek the blessings of Skanda-Murukan (Shiva's son) at Kataragama.

Pilgrims from four faiths make the ascent to a mountaintop forty-five miles (seventy-five kilometers) east of Colombo, the conical Adam's Peak rising over 8,000 feet (2,500 meters). They may start out on the back of a bullock cart or even in a vehicle, but they accomplish the last few hours of the climb on foot. Refreshment stalls along the route assist the weary and—if it is a daytime pilgrimage—the heat-stricken. At the top is an enclosure with several small buildings and a flat boulder that has an indentation like a footprint. This is the object they seek.

FOOTPRINTS IN TIME

To Buddhists, this rock is the Place of the Sacred Footprint because it is where the Buddha once stood to teach his followers the way to Enlightenment. To Hindus, the footprint is Shiva's, who made it when he danced the Dance of Creation at the beginning of the world. To Muslims, on the other hand, the Place of the Sacred

ABOVE: *While live elephants have a crucial role to play in the principal forms of Buddhist ceremonies at Kataragama, their carved stone relations are integral to the adornment of the temple there.*

Footprint is where Adam first walked upon the Earth. And Christians, who accord it the least antiquity, claim the footprint is that of Christ's apostle St. Thomas, said to have preached in southern India after the Crucifixion and the Resurrection.

Pilgrims from all these faiths come to Adam's peak in the later months of the year. To the east of the peak lies the equally venerated and ancient site

of Kataragama. It, too, is a destination visited, most often in July and August, by Hindus, Muslims, Christians, and Buddhists, along with Westerners simply seeking enlightenment in a New Age. The deity most closely associated with Kataragama is the Hindu god Skanda-Murukan, at whose temple visitors from these other faiths also pray and make their offerings. A mile or so away is the official Buddhist shrine, where the Buddha is believed to have meditated. Also at the site is a mosque commemorating the Sufi saint al-Khizr. Many names have been used to invoke the original deity of

Kataragama, whose feats are celebrated in so many languages—Sanskrit and Tamil for Hindus, Pali and Sinhala for Buddhists—and to whom pilgrims come in often extreme circumstances.

HINDU KATARAGAMA

Of all the pilgrimages to Kataragama, the most astonishing is also undoubtedly the most ancient. Traditionally starting from the island's far north and ending up to two months and several hundred kilometers later at the Kataragama shrine in the remote southeastern jungle, the *Pada Yatra* (foot pilgrimage) tradition probably predates the arrival

of all four of Sri Lanka's major religions and is inherited from the island's indigenous forest dwellers the Wanniya or Vedda. Braving hunger and thirst, scorching sun and pouring rain, people walk barefoot through stretches of jungle infested with poisonous plants, wild beasts, and robbers. Some die en route. Such a death has over the years been reckoned an exceptional distinction for which many have prayed fervently.

Pilgrims usually travel in groups headed by a group leader known as the Vel Swami because he carries the *vel* or spear, the weapon of Lord Skanda-Murukan. He would have performed the pilgrimage himself in earlier years and is therefore

expected to direct the group along the confusing forest routes on the way. Traditionally, a group consisted of around thirty people; but in recent years, for security reasons, the number is larger. The pilgrims pray at many important temples along the way before reaching Kataragama.

In the Tamil language, the Kataragama Pada Yatra is known as *Katira Malai kar ai yattirai*, the "coastal pilgrimage to the Shining Peak." Like his "father" Shiva, Skanda-Murukan is a god associated with mountains and hilltops.

Among the Tamil Hindus in the pilgrim bands are Sinhalese Buddhists and Muslim pilgrims, along with a few Westerners—possibly a thousand people make the trek each year. The recent Tamil political emergencies and civil unrest have considerably restricted the numbers going from the northern areas. Most pilgrims to Kataragama now come from Sri Lanka's eastern districts, itself a feat but not quite as arduous as the long trek from the north of the island. Pilgrims tend to start out from relatively developed and ordered communities, but as they move south, the towns and villages get smaller and farther apart until the pilgrims must

RIGHT: The long and often weary ascent to the top of Adam's Peak is undertaken in the latter part of the year by a steady stream of pilgrims from four different faiths.

cross fifty miles (eighty kilometers) of uninhabited jungle, the Yala National Park and its environs. When they arrive, some of the pilgrims complete their pain-filled journey by walking on hot coals.

BUDDHIST KATARAGAMA

Followers of each religion debate whether the god is really a Hindu or Buddhist deity. Skanda-Murukan is also venerated by Sri Lanka's Christians and indeed some of its Muslims, who invoke the deity with their intercessions. The Sri Lankans tend to swallow their differences in the end—the form of Kataragama's worship is a rich cross-fertilization. Numerically, however, most of his devotees are Sinhalese Buddhists. Rather than being genuinely divine, Kataragama is, for Buddhists, a great *bodhisattva* or once-human "being of enlightenment" vested with extraordinary ability to help those who appeal to him.

Many Buddhist pilgrims to the site do not follow a set ritual, in keeping with precepts of their beliefs. Some light a lamp and burn incense; others give alms to the monks or offer flowers. The faithful may recite some of the Buddha's sayings. Some doubtless ponder on the Eightfold Path to Enlightenment—right understanding, right state of mind, right speech, right actions, right livelihood, right endeavors, right-mindedness, and right concentration on things that benefit the mind. Each follows his or her own route toward *nirvana*—or "state of bliss"—for the religion that Prince Gautama founded was one without theology, temples, sacrifice, priests, or sacred books. (Over time, it acquired most of these, beginning with the domed *stupas* beneath which were buried relics of the Buddha himself. It also swiftly acquired different "denominations," beginning with the original split between the austere Theravada and the more worldly Mahayana Buddhists.)

However, some Buddhists perform grand rituals at Kataragama, as well as personal forms of prayer. The *Esala Perahera* is the ritual progress conducted nightly during the waxing moon of Esala (July–August) involving lamplight processions around the mountains and to the rivers. The Esala festival reaches its climax on the evening of the full moon, when the life and works of the ancient Sinhalese king Masahena, a great protector of Buddhism, are celebrated. A colorful torchlit procession moves at a stately pace along the path to nearby Kirivehera: one trained elephant carries on its back a casket-reliquary symbolizing the Lord Buddha's presence, while another follows carrying King Mahasena as symbolized by his six-angled *yantra* device, a geometric pattern that helps inspire prayer. The monks of Kirivehera receive the chief official who "accepts the five cardinal precepts" (not to kill, steal, fornicate, lie, or drink intoxicants), and the eight permitted drinks are offered as refreshment for the Lord and his monastic community. It may not be considered "orthodox," but this ritual incorporates what are possibly millennia-old concerns and observances.

ISLAND OF SERENDIPITY

"Oh pilgrim!," the local Buddhist text says, "Listen to the call however faint it may be, and if none comes along to join you, walk alone." Pilgrims to Kataragama tend to be far from alone. They have tradition on their side. The word "serendipity," making happy discoveries by accident, comes from *Serendib*, the name that Arab seafarers once gave to this island, since called Ceylon and now Sri Lanka. It has been for thousands of years a sacred destination for pilgrims of many religious persuasions. Christians rub shoulders with Buddhists, Muslims, and Hindus. Their devotions may be separate but their zeal for spiritual discovery is not diminished.

Prayer flags are part of the Buddhist tradition, but they have also been taken up by other faiths in southern Sri Lanka as part of the repertoire of invocation and prayer.

A monk adds incense sticks to the ceremonial fire in one of the round of festivals that draw pilgrims to the Shinto and Buddhist shrines and temples of Japan's old imperial capital.

JOURNEY TEN

Kyoto

MODERN TRAVELERS MAY *speed from Tokyo, Japan's modern capital, to Kyoto, the old imperial capital city, in a matter of hours on one of the famous* shinkansen, *the so-called bullet trains. In earlier centuries the most popular road in the nation for both pleasure and religion was this same route, the Tokaido Road between Edo (Tokyo's old name) and Kyoto. It is a distance of 340 miles (550 kilometers), and there were numerous "stations" on the route—fifty-seven in total—that were both resting places and religious shrines.*

JAPAN

Tokyo

Yokohama

Kyoto
Osaka

Hiroshima

SHIKOKU

KYUSHU

The great woodblock artist Hokusai in 1818 published a map and a series of views along the Tokaido Road, such as the waterfall at Sakanoshita. There pilgrims would ascend the stone steps alongside the Kiyotaki, the "pure waterfall" with its exceptionally clear stream, to a shrine to the Buddhist goddess Kannon. This waterfall and the deity are still visited, as are the gardens, shrines, and temples of old Kyoto at journey's end. Behind the modern outlook, age-old observances remain at the heart of Japanese culture.

TWO PATHS

Japan's two principal religions, Shinto and Buddhism, are inextricably intertwined. The Shinto *kami* (superior spirits) inhabit rocks, trees, water, and wayside shrines that are also among the building blocks of Buddhist belief. Pilgrims may go to a shrine or a temple for a particular purpose, but often in both religions the very action of going, following a circuit and contemplating a natural feature, is quite as important as the outcome. A Japanese pilgrim may not always have a specific goal in the Western sense, but accomplishes a sense of religious achievement in performing a ritual or contemplating a particular stone, tree, or waterfall. According to a religious survey undertaken in Japan in the early 1990s, 107 million Japanese people claim affiliation to a Shinto organization.

BELOW: The Kinkaku-ji, or Golden Pavilion, is one of Kyoto's most celebrated Buddhist temples. Its walls are covered in gold leaf, and it is set within one of the finest contemplative temple gardens.

And 96 million claim affiliation to a Buddhist organization. Yet the total population of Japan is 124 million. This situation could hardly be further from the denominational demarcation lines of the Christian West. Visits to both temples (the English word ordinarily used for Buddhist holy places, known locally as *tera*) and shrines (used for Shinto sites, known locally as *jinja* or *jinshu*) are an integral part of Japanese culture. The Japanese are not practicing a pick-and-mix form of religion and they are not simply trying to hedge their bets. Rather, the two separate faith systems respond to different aspects of their lives.

The native pantheistic religion of Japan became known as Shinto (the way of the gods) in the sixth century AD to distinguish it from a newly arrived religion, Buddhism. The Indian Prince Siddhartha Gautama—the Buddha—founded Buddhism in the fifth century BC. But the belief system that reached Japan a thousand years later came from China and Korea. These East Asian varieties, with their additional gods and attached elements, are different in many respects from the Buddhism that stems directly from India.

The two sets of belief coexist in modern Japan. A typical young Japanese man or woman probably has few religious beliefs—but he or she would not visit a temple or a shrine without going through the traditional ritual of cleansing, clapping, bowing, and making offerings. Shinto rituals are commonly

BELOW: Many of the festivals that people come to mark in Kyoto are concerned with the deep reverence for aged members of the family and for their ancestors.

used for weddings and festivals—auspicious events in personal or communal life. Buddhist temples are usually the setting for solemn and transcendent occasions, notably funerals. The two systems have usually been tolerant of one another in fifteen hundred years of mutual interdependence.

Nowhere is the symbiosis more visible than in the city of Kyoto. The shrines, temples, worship halls, palaces, castles, and gardens within the city and in the mountains around it are the finest of their kind anywhere. Many of the people who visit are tourists, and, while they are not pilgrims in the accepted Western sense of the word, most of them could be considered pilgrims in a wider, Japanese view of the world. However, visits to the shrines and temples will always be overwhelmingly religious experiences for some people.

EMPEROR AND SHOGUN

The Japanese classical period, or the Heian era, began in 785 when the imperial capital was established at the new city of Heian-kyo, later known as Kyoto. That era ended in 1185 when Minamato no Yoritomo seized power over the emperor and the long rule of the shogunate began. Kyoto remained the imperial capital for the next seven hundred years and was principally a ceremonial center. The *shogun*, the military dictator of Japan, had his main castle in Edo (now Tokyo). In a feudal society, the shogun had power in each region over the *daimio*—a provincial feudal lord answerable to him—while the samurai were members of the aristocratic military class serving their daimio. The shogun was only nominally subservient to the emperor until the final overthrow of the shogunate in 1868, when Tokyo became the imperial capital.

It was in this climate of warlords and feudal society that the hundreds, if not thousands, of temples and shrines flourished in Kyoto. Although fire

has ravaged many ancient structures, which were built principally in wood, some buildings do still survive from the Heian era. Some sites receive a myriad of visitors and pilgrims on a daily basis; others are barely known to the world at large.

RELIGIOUS CELEBRATION AND RITUAL

Shinto is a celebration of life rather than a belief, in which fertility rites have always taken the most prominent place. Those fertility rites are both human and agricultural. The religion has its origins in rice farming: the original deities were the sun, the storm, and the mountains, rivers, and lakes that collected and supplied the water for irrigation. Ancestors and revered men from the past retain a prominent place. Shinto also became a cult centered on the emperor and the imperial family, a form of the religion that received its ultimate expression in the "State Shinto" of the period from the 1860s to the 1940s, but that was suppressed after Japan's defeat in World War II.

Although State Shinto has gone, the basic beliefs and attitudes persist, notably in the passion for cleanliness and purification that runs through Japanese society and in the reverence and awe for nature. Shinto observances have their most obvious expression in the *matsuri*—festivals that may be local, regional, or national in scope, and decorous or uproarious in character. The New Year in the old calendar, for example, celebrated on February 2–3, involves demon dancers and fire at Kyoto's shrines and temples. The Yoshino Mountains near Kyoto have always particularly attracted visitors during April, the third month of the lunar calendar, because that is when beautiful cherry trees are in blossom. Hokusai, the celebrated woodblock artist, captured the scene two hundred years ago in a print showing pilgrims approaching a Shinto shrine on the mountain,

ascending through a sea of white cherry blossom. Modern pilgrimages to view the blossom become a weeklong drinking bout, while in October the gaudy processions of the Festival of the Ages and the Fire Festival, Jidai Matsuri and Hi-matsuri, attract thousands of participants.

Few areas of Japanese culture remain untouched by Buddhism, the second great religious influence on the nation. In their long transformation from the religion founded in fifth-century BC India, the Japanese forms of Buddhism—Zen, perhaps being the most famous—are themselves distinctive sects that have evolved incorporating Shinto-derived and other beliefs. A complex system of deities centers on the four *Nyorai* (Buddhas)—including the historical Buddha—flanked by *Bosatsu* (Bodhisattvas in

ABOVE: Prayers and invocations written on paper scrolls are tied to the branches of cherry trees in flower. The blossom season every April is one of the busiest times of the year for visiting Kyoto's sacred sites— both natural and man-made.

Indian terminology). The Bosatsu are beings of great spiritual merit who have chosen to defer enlightenment in order to save others.

Kannon is the foremost of these great beings — originally a Hindu god with an over-rounded body transformed in China and Japan into a Buddhist goddess of compassion and mercy. The greatest of Kyoto's temples devoted to Kannon is the Sanjusangen-do, where a thousand gilded statues of the deity stand in a hundred diagonal rows, each ten statues deep. On January 15 every year since 1606, a kind of pilgrimage event has taken place at

Sanjusangen-do in the form of an archery contest. The Japanese devotees use arrows to carry their prayers and invocations, just as candle flames are used at Catholic shrines.

In Kyoto's To-ji temple, the last lively Buddhist festival of the old year and the first of a new takes place on December 21 and January 21 to commemorate the revered eighth-century saint and teacher Kukai, founder of the Shingon sect and known posthumously as Kobo Daishi. (Kukai's greatest celebration takes place on the island of Shikoku, where Zen adherents visit eighty-eight stations on a great circular pilgrimage.)

In rather more sombre mood, on August 7–10 families embark on the annual Rokudo pilgrimage to welcome the spirits of the dead with lanterns and gongs. These ceremonies take place in temples near Kiyomizu-dera, once a cemetery area.

A week later, O-bon, the festival of the dead, ends at Daimonji when families come to honor the spirits of their dead ancestors and five great bonfires are lit on the mountains that surround Kyoto. At the full moon in September, moon-viewing ceremonies take place at the imperial shrines of Daikaku-ji and Uji.

PILGRIM WAYS

The greatest of the Shinto shrines, Fushimi Inari Taisha, stands on the side of Mount Inari, southeast of central Kyoto. It is dedicated to Inari, god of rice and hence of money and prosperity. Founded in the eighth century, and with buildings that date back to the fifteenth century, it is one of the oldest surviving shrines in Japan. The mountain is covered with secondary shrines, and the pilgrim paths that lead up the slopes to the mountaintop are bridged by thousands of red *torii* (gates), clustered close together to form tunnels. These gates are corporate-tax deductible, and they bear the names of

the companies that erected them seeking divine favour. Dotted around are the carved figures of foxes, guardians of the shrine; smaller ceramic versions are for sale in the pilgrim shops that are clustered together almost as closely as the torii.

Neither Fushimi Inari Taisha nor Heian Jungu, the State Shinto shrine of 1894 to the Heian emperors, ever closes. However, many of Kyoto's smaller and secondary temples—such as Anraku-ji, where the Buddhist Jodo sect was founded; Reikan-ji, the small imperial convent; and Daitoku-ji, the great Zen temple complex—are open only a few days during the year. Visitors are usually welcome in early November, when pilgrims come from all over to see the maple and gingko trees in their spectacular autumn colors and to contemplate beauty and evanescence.

Daitoku-ji also possesses one of the great, classic Japanese gardens that are such a feature of Kyoto's temples: this one is a miniature translation in gravel, stone, and minimal planting of a Chinese Sung landscape. It was a collaboration between the monastery's founding priest Kogaku and the artist Soami in the fourteenth century, and has been both an inspiration and a place for pilgrim contemplation ever since.

Contemplating a beautiful garden of raked gravel, climbing beside a waterfall, enjoying the beauty of nature—these are aspects that make pilgrimage distinctive in Japan, even compared with, say, those parts of Portugal where religious observance and pilgrim journeys are an integral part of everyday life. Although many pilgrims to the shrines and temples, cherry trees, and hillsides of the former imperial capital may not appreciate the nuances of their activities, they are self-consciously adhering to age-old tradition. They follow in the footsteps of the many generations that went before them, and they observe the same sets of rituals that link them to their ancestors.

The torii gates over the pilgrim paths on the side of Mount Inari cluster so thickly together that they form tunnels. This is one of the oldest shrines in Japan and it still thrives.

Soaring in the middle of the Pyrenean mountains, the vast basilica at Lourdes that marks the site of the appearances of the Virgin Mary to St. Bernadette in 1858 is one of the greatest destinations for pilgrims in the modern Christian world.

JOURNEY ELEVEN

Lourdes

ABOVE: *Bernadette Soubirous, the young French woman to whom a vision of the Virgin Mary appeared.*

PILGRIMAGES TO LOURDES *are on a scale the world barely otherwise sees. Pilgrims both ill and healthy come by bus, train, and plane—a few on foot—to share in the wonder. A little town in southwestern France, Lourdes is one of the Christian world's greatest pilgrimage shrines.*

Almost two thirds of Europe's religious shrines are for Mary. There are nearly four thousand of them—ten times those devoted to Jesus. Astride the great medieval pilgrim routes into Spain, the Lourdes region of southwestern France had long been steeped in tales of miracles and of the Virgin Mary's loving mercy and power. Then in 1858, a young French peasant had a vision that was to make her and her hometown of Lourdes famous: Bernadette Soubirous, a poor and barely literate girl of fourteen, saw a shining apparition who eventually identified herself as the Immaculate Conception and indicated the source of a spring with healing properties. The wonder of Lourdes had begun. Now a shrine indelibly associated with miraculous cures, Lourdes is a symbol of hope throughout the Catholic world.

A FLOOD OF PILGRIMS

At first Lourdes was merely a national center for penitence, healing, and remorse. But in 1873, the first pilgrimages arrived from Canada and Belgium and were soon followed by others from the United States, Poland, Italy, Germany, Brazil, Hungary, and Britain. By now, Lourdes has received visitors from all over the world. Around eight million people arrived during the centenary of Bernadette's visions in 1958; and while no other year has produced those numbers, the tide of humanity washing upon the small Pyrenean town has been vast. Around five million people still visit Lourdes annually. It is now possible to make a virtual pilgrimage by logging on to the Internet at www.lourdes-france.com, where one may hear the sounds of the town bells as they ring out the Lourdes hymn, "Ave! Ave! Ave Maria!" A series of view cams provide constantly updated pictures, day and night, of the grotto and the main basilica.

BERNADETTE'S VISIONS

It was on February 11, 1858, that Bernadette had the first of her eighteen visions of Mary. Already ill herself with the tuberculosis that would eventually kill her, Bernadette accompanied her sister and a friend to look for wood on a sandy area beside the River Gave de Pau, known as Massabielle. Before wading across the river, she heard a wind and then saw a soft light coming from a niche in a grotto. A beautiful, smiling child in white seemed to beckon to her. Startled, Bernadette reached for her rosary; the apparition then reached for her own rosary. Slowly the vision faded away. Nobody else saw anything—nobody else was ever to see anything.

The vision returned twice more and then spoke to Bernadette in her native dialect, asking her to come back over the next fifteen days. As news spread, more people accompanied Bernadette and saw her face transfigured as she communed with the apparition. The civil authorities' attempts both to get Bernadette to confess it was a hoax and to restrict access to the site failed. Bernadette never gave a name to what she saw, referring to the vision only as *Aquéro* (that thing.) During the ninth apparition, Bernadette started scrabbling at the earth and drinking dirty water she found there. Onlookers were shocked, until a spring appeared at the site. She received instructions in the thirteenth apparition that the priests should come to the grotto and build a chapel. The parish priest wanted a sign from the apparition—the girl should make a rose bush bloom and give Bernadette her name. No sign was given, no name was mentioned, and the fifteen-day cycle ended. Then three weeks later, on March 25, the Feast of the Annunciation, Bernadette went back. Finally, the vision gave its name: "I am the Immaculate Conception."

Bernadette's divine mission was soon over. The sanctuary passed into more orthodox, ecclesiastical hands. Even the vision she had—of a child about

Our Lady of Lourdes has become one of the most potent and popular emblems of Catholicism since the mid-nineteenth century. Bernadette said the image was not quite the same apparition she had seen, but accepted that the Church wanted an adult figure.

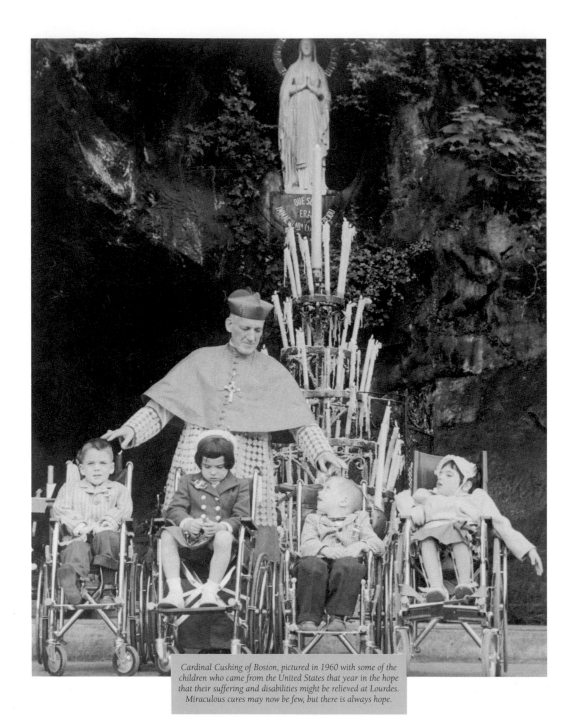

Cardinal Cushing of Boston, pictured in 1960 with some of the children who came from the United States that year in the hope that their suffering and disabilities might be relieved at Lourdes. Miraculous cures may now be few, but there is always hope.

ABOVE: *The spires on the main Basilica of the Rosary symbolize the prayers and supplications of the faithful going heavenward. In order to accommodate ever-rising numbers of pilgrims and to avoid over filling the site, the modern basilica of 1958 was built underground.*

her own age—was transformed into the mature woman that is immediately recognizable as Our Lady of Lourdes. People were soon making claims that the water Bernadette had uncovered had miraculous healing properties, and while Lourdes developed into one of the greatest of all Christian shrines, the visionary herself entered a convent and spent most of the rest of her painful and short life away in central France. She died in Nevers in 1878, and her embalmed body lies in a reliquary there rather than in Lourdes.

LOURDES PROSPERS

Bernadette's story has the quality of a fairy tale. Yet nothing was inevitable about the success of Lourdes. Its visionary came from a poor and disreputable family, in a remote part of France where sacred visions were not uncommon. The apparition gave few signs and uttered only minimal messages, the most important—"I am the Immaculate Conception"—being enigmatic. The civil authorities did their best to prevent a shrine from being established. Yet Lourdes prospered through a happy combination of events, and within twenty years hundreds of thousands of pilgrims, rich and poor, were going to the shrine from all over France. Within another twenty years it had become an international phenomenon.

ABOVE: *Lourdes was to become the great shrine of the age of trains, for until recent times the vast majority of pilgrims would have come by train from all over France and the rest of Europe. Air and road travel have overtaken rail, but many of the ill still come on special trains.*

What cemented the success of Lourdes was the railroad. The opening of the line in 1866 made this remote place suddenly accessible from across the nation. Although most pilgrims now come by bus and plane, for over a century the train was the principal means of travel (and special trains remain a favored way of transporting the terminally ill). The doctrine of the Immaculate Conception—that Mary was untainted by Original Sin the instant following her conception—had only just been made official dogma in 1854. The apparition's pronouncement was therefore conveniently timed for the Church authorities. Among the very early visitors to the shrine seeking healing were the governess of the ailing Prince Imperial, son of Louis Napoleon and Eugénie, and Louis Veuillot, then France's most influential Catholic layman and journalist. With the ease of access provided by the railroad, and the apparent endorsements of the Church, the monarchy, and the press, Lourdes was set on its path to renown.

Fulfilling the vision's request, the first church—the Basilica of the Immaculate Conception—was built beside the grotto between 1864 and 1874. From then on, orthodoxy weighed heavily on the fragile natural setting of the apparitions. A second church, the Basilica of the Rosary, with its curious mixture of Romano–Byzantine architectural styles, rose slowly toward the end of the nineteenth century. Begun in 1883, it incorporated ramps to transport the sick, a vast esplanade to accommodate the pilgrims, and the *Asile*, a hospital for the very ill. When these buildings could no longer contain the increasing number of visitors, a third and great underground basilica was completed in time for the centenary celebrations.

IN HOPE OF THE MIRACULOUS

A pilgrimage organizer has a huge task in booking transportation, securing accommodations, and ensuring that medical care is available for the sick, some of whom may be terminally ill and unused to arduous travel. The journey to Lourdes is often conducted in a mixture of piety and warmth, as those who are well are encouraged to assist in the care of those less fortunate. Many modern pilgrims come as part of organized groups, on pilgrimage with others from their local diocese or archdiocese. The sick may have a residual hope that they will receive a miraculous cure, but none dares feel confident of that unlikely event. The closeness and the spiritual warmth are usually quite sufficient.

Arriving at Lourdes along with many thousands of others can be a bewildering, overwhelming, and yet uplifting experience. The casual or unbelieving visitor is often shocked by the religious kitsch on sale: super-sized rosaries or saints that glow in the dark, plaster statuettes, wall plaques, and plastic containers of every shape for spring water. For those caught up in the pilgrimage, attending to the needs of the sick and the dying, these souvenirs are irrelevant and go unnoticed. In any event, the souvenir stalls are excluded from the *domaine*, the sacred area close to the grotto where the basilicas are located and pilgrimage activities are centered.

Healing is at the very heart of the Lourdes experience. Bodies in pain are made spiritual by the ritual round of the pilgrimage, the eucharistic

ABOVE: Our Lady of Lourdes, "At the cross her station keeping. . . ." Pilgrims follow the traditional Stations of the Cross set among the rocky outcrops in the domaine, *close to the rock of Massabielle where Bernadette had her visions and where the miracles began.*

processions and bathing in the freezing waters of the pools. Cures for the incurable, solace for the tormented—these were the hopes that were raised by the visions and the spring that Bernadette had discovered. Cures were claimed almost as soon as the water had been found, and the trickle of miracles—the lame walking, the blind seeing—soon turned into a flood. At the 1897 pilgrimage, marking twenty-five years of national pilgrimage to Lourdes, 325 surviving *miraculés* were present, men and—especially—women who had received cures at the shrine or with its waters. The pressure on the Church to submit these claims to scientific inquiry had already led to the foundation in 1883 of the Lourdes Medical Bureau, intended to subject every supposed miracle to rigorous scrutiny.

The scrutiny is now so rigorous that no miracle has been proclaimed for more than a generation. Most recently, in February 1999 the bishop of Angoulême, France, announced that the cure from multiple sclerosis that Jean-Pierre Bély had experienced at Lourdes twelve years earlier, was "truly a sign of Christ," drawing short of proclaiming it a full-scale miracle.

In fact, of the sixty-four cures officially recognized as miraculous, twenty-six occurred before 1900. The diseases include tuberculosis, cancer, blindness, and paralysis. Still they come—the infirm and their helpers. Even without the Church's endorsement of recent cures, many of the world's faithful do claim relief, and even healing, from their visit to Lourdes.

THE RITUAL ROUND

The pattern of ritual events was established at an early stage and has remained little-altered ever since. Many of the hostels, *pensions*, and hotels that cater for pilgrims date their origins back to the

nineteenth century, and they are crowded through the long pilgrim season. Although the curative effects of the water may now be deemphasized, the ritual of the bath remains part of the Lourdes experience. Thousands will bathe each day during the busiest pilgrimages, the ice-cold water in the baths being replenished regularly. The very sick bathe at separate times from the able bodied, and those who are less seriously ill take precedence over the healthy. Men and women stand in separate lines. They inch forward until they reach the bathing pool. *Brancardiers*—the porters who are the dedicated lay helpers of the sick—are at hand to get the pilgrims in and out of the water and to keep the process running as smoothly as possible. As one pilgrim removes his or her clothes, another crouches in the freezing water saying the prescribed prayer, and a third is dressing again, pulling dry clothes onto wet body.

ABOVE: It is a vast undertaking to bring the millions of pilgrims to this mountainside location, especially since many of them are extremely ill. The sense of hope, faith, and togetherness is palpable at Lourdes, especially at the hours of bathing and the Blessing of the Sick.

The cycle of masses begins in the early afternoon, now in a Babel of languages where once only Latin would have been heard. Sometimes, pilgrim groups will take their devotions up into the beautiful encircling hills. The climax comes at 4:30 P.M. with the Blessed Sacrament procession and the ceremony of the Blessing of the Sick.

Finally, as night falls, the torchlight procession makes its way to the grotto with thousands upon thousands of pilgrims carrying their candles and flaming lights, singing the Lourdes hymn—one of the defining features of Lourdes. Miracles are hard to come by in the twenty-first century, but there are many who still come to Lourdes in hope.

Wearing the dress prescribed in the Koran, the ihram for men and appropriately decorous apparel for women, Muslims assemble in Mecca by the million each year for the hajj pilgrimage, which is one of the Pillars of their faith.

JOURNEY TWELVE

Mecca and the Hajj

IN ENGLISH, THE very word mecca has come to mean "something aspired to," "a goal,"—a dream to be fulfilled. To a Muslim, Mecca is a great deal more than a dream for fulfillment. It is a place of fulfillment, a sacred space to which only the faithful may be admitted. Worshippers around the world at the appointed hours of prayer turn toward Mecca and prostrate themselves before Allah, the one true God.

ABOVE: *Following rituals ordained by the Koran and hallowed by well over a thousand years of ritual observance since the days of the Prophet, pilgrims to Mecca reach out to Allah.*

Unlike in any of the other great religions, in Islam pilgrimage is not just a spiritual opportunity but a spiritual obligation. The *hajj*—the journey to Mecca, birthplace of the Prophet Muhammad (Mohammed), and performing there a prescribed set of rituals—is one of the five "Pillars of Islam." These observances are what make a believer into a full Muslim.

HAJJ

Mecca itself lies in an inhospitable strip of land, the Hijaz, on the east coast of the Red Sea in modern Saudi Arabia. Today, as travel becomes easier and incomes have risen, each year many millions of Muslims make the hajj, almost overwhelming this tiny corner of the Arab world. In previous centuries it was the preserve of the most devout, the most determined, and those with the greatest wealth, and a *hajji*—someone who had returned

ABOVE and RIGHT: Pressure of numbers may overwhelm the routes and the great mosque itself, but the hajj is still as much a personal as well as a collective demonstration of faith.

ABOVE: *Of the half-million pilgrims that the Sacred Mosque can hold, only a lucky few will be able to get close enough to touch the sacred black stone of the Ka'aba, which was the shrine built by Abraham.*

from Mecca—was a person revered for the rest of his life. It would once have been unheard of to perform the hajj more than once. Today it is far from uncommon. Yet every pilgrim is asked by family, friends, and even strangers to add their prayers to his or hers at Mecca.

A whole industry in and beyond Saudi Arabia revolves around the annual pilgrimage. Platoons of health-care professionals inoculate pilgrims before they embark on their journey. Pilgrims haggle with travel agencies that specialize in hajj journeys. Air-traffic control and port control for shipping in Jeddah and elsewhere in Saudi Arabia are stretched beyond capacity, while special border posts have to be maintained to cope with those who travel over-

land in the traditional way, especially the poor of Arabia and the very devout. The roads everywhere are jammed with vehicles. Specially built accommodations and tent cities surround the sacred places, and a vast housing estate, the Pilgrims' City, has been built close to Jeddah airport solely for use on a few days a year.

Buses and taxis are required by the thousand to ferry the pilgrims from place to place. Guides swarm everywhere, as do security agents—for no non-Muslim may enter the sacred sites. Medical services are in constant attendance, as there are many deaths every day from natural causes among the millions of pilgrims. A substantial number of accidental deaths have occurred—more than one hundred at the 2001 hajj alone—in the crush of visitors or when buildings have collapsed under the sheer weight of humanity. On occasion disputes between different branches of Islam have even erupted into hostility and open violence. Oil-rich Saudi Arabia has waived the payments it is entitled to collect from Muslim nations for hosting the ceremonies, so it is a drain on the public purse.

THE PROPHET AND HIS CITY

Muhammad received a final revelation from God—"final" in the sense that parts of the message had already been revealed to Moses and Jesus—in the seventh century AD. God's message was written in Arabic in the *Koran* (or Qur'an) (the Perfect Book.) Allah, the One true God of Islam, chose the Arabian peninsula as the origin of the world; that is where He placed Adam, and when He commanded Abraham to leave Syria, Abraham built a shrine in the unfruitful desert valley of the Hijaz. This shrine became known as the *Ka'aba* (cube.) In the intervening centuries the shrine had been taken over for the worship of pagan idols, and Muhammad saw it as his task to expel their worship from the site and restore the shrine to Allah.

The life and practice of the Prophet became the basis of a true Muslim life. Allah is to be proclaimed the one true God and Muhammad his prophet. Muslims recite prayers five times a day. The faithful are to fast during daylight hours in the holy month of Ramadan, and they are exhorted to give alms. Crucially, once in a lifetime, a Muslim should perform the *hajj*, the pilgrimage to Mecca, provided funds and health permit.

Muhammad himself, who came from a middling mercantile family, began to preach in around 610, when he was forty. His denunciation of the worship of idols and his passionate adherence to monotheistic beliefs threatened the commercial livelihood of his birthplace, because the town depended heavily on the trade from the annual religious gatherings. Finally Muhammad and his followers fled to the nearby city of Medina in 622,

and the year of his exile became the date on which the Muslim era began. From Medina he waged a war of economic attrition on Mecca, and in 630 the city capitulated, the old gods and idols were destroyed and the Ka'aba was purified. In 632, just before his death, Muhammad went on pilgrimage to Mecca, in the footsteps of both Adam and Abraham. Around 100,000 new believers followed him and heard him speak his final words in public.

After the Prophet's death, the followers of Islam embarked on a program of conquest throughout the Middle East and North Africa, and then further afield. They were now united by religion rather than divided by tribal loyalties. In 660 the center of Muslim organization shifted to Damascus, and Mecca became what it has been ever since, a place focused almost solely on the *hajj*. In later centuries, Mecca itself became a political and religious football as the Muslim world split between Sunni, Sufi, and Shi'ite adherents. In the eighteenth century zealots cleansed the hajj of secular excesses, and their influence remains in the strict emphasis on correct performance of the prescribed rituals.

THE RITUALS

The word *hajj* means "an effort," and whether in the former days of camel trains across the desert or modern times when the aircraft are stacked above Jeddah airport waiting to land, it has always been an effort. There are some 700 million Muslims in the world today, and only a fraction of them will ever be able to go to Mecca. Yet that fraction is far greater now than it was a generation ago, and is far, far greater than in earlier centuries. It now means that usually two million people make the annual pilgrimage—and they all go at the same time.

The Islamic community of faith is the *umma*, and the thoughts and prayers of the whole umma will be with those who have reached Mecca.

ABOVE: Pilgrims each select forty-nine small stones, seven by seven, before they leave Arafat. This was the place where the Prophet delivered his last sermon and is an integral point on the hajj circuit.

Inasmuch as only Muslims may enter the holy city and photographs have only been allowed in recent years, the exclusivity of the Islamic experience is pronounced.

The focus of attention at Mecca is the Ka'aba, which dates largely from the seventh century, although it has been much restored. Within its east corner is embedded the sacred black stone, a meteorite that is believed to be a relic from the days of Adam and Abraham. It was certainly a focus of ritual attention in the pre-Islamic days of idol worship. Fragments of the buildings around it date back to the time of Muhammad. The cube is never revealed but is covered with the *kiswah*, a black cloth on which verses from scripture are embroidered in gold.

The hajj occurs between the eighth and thirteenth days of the twelfth month in the Muslim calendar. Corresponding to a lunar rather than a solar calendar, the dates shift from year to year in a regular cycle. First, the Muslim identity of the pilgrim must be established. Before pilgrims pass the boundary stones marking the edge of the sacred territory, they vow to abstain from worldly actions while they are there: they may not cut their hair or their nails, they must not have sexual intercourse, they must remain in amicable agreement with their neighbors and they must not adorn their bodies with perfume or jewelry. Men wear the *ihram*—two plain white sheets without seams, one around the

waist and one draped over the shoulder—and shoes without stitching. Women dress decorously, but their dress is not so closely prescribed. Specially appointed guides assist the pilgrims throughout the complex sequence of devotions.

After arriving at the great courtyard of the Sacred Mosque in which the Ka'aba stands, the pilgrim kisses the black stone—although pressure of numbers now usually means that he or she simply waves at it or calls out to it from a distance. The pilgrims walk around it seven times—the *tuwaf*. When they pray here it will be the only time in their lives that they do not all face in one direction —toward Mecca—for they *are* at Mecca, their highest goal on earth, and so the half-million pilgrims that the Sacred Mosque holds arrange themselves in concentric circles centered on the Ka'aba.

ABOVE: At Mina, pilgrims stone the three pillars as a physical commemoration of the actions of Abraham who, according to tradition, thus chased away the devil and his wicked temptations.

Then they perform the *sa'y*: running between two hillocks, al-Safa and al-Marwa, seven times to commemorate the actions of Abraham's wife Hagar as she searched for water for their son Ishmael. The 500-yard (460-meter) route is no longer a stony track but an air-conditioned colonnade, with one-way traffic on each pathway to ease the congestion. The holy well of Zamzam is still located within the sacred courtyard, and the bitter water from it is eagerly drunk or bottled and taken home.

Next follows one of the most important parts of the hajj, which takes place not in Mecca itself but at the Mount of Mercy in Arafat, on the barren

Darkness falls, but the observances at Mecca's Sacred Mosque continue as pilgrims walk around the Ka'aba seven times in the ritual of the tawaf before prostrating themselves in prayer.

plain some eleven miles (eighteen kilometers) east. This was where the Prophet delivered his last sermon. A whole day, "the day of standing before God," is devoted to prayer and fasting at the Mosque of Namira, but then the pilgrims must hasten away before the hour of final prayers at nightfall. It is an almost unseemly rush as fleets of buses and taxis attempt to leave Arafat all at the same time. Before they leave, the pilgrims select forty-nine small stones. They will use them for the stoning of the three pillars at the tiny town of Mina, temporarily transformed into a tent city, over the following three days: the days of *tashriq*. This stoning ceremony does not actually follow a Koranic text, but it is said to memorialize the occasion when Abraham hurled stones at the devil, who was tempting him to disobey God's will when he was forced to offer his son for sacrifice. Again, specially built walkways accommodate all the pilgrims as they pass to and fro.

Ritual slaughter of animals for food follows, a sacrifice in which Muslims all around the world join at the same time. In light of the numbers of pilgrims, more than a million lambs and kids are prepared for the butcher's knife. There is far more food than the pilgrims could ever hope to consume or give away in alms, and disposal of the carcasses is a source of major embarrassment to the Saudi Arabian authorities.

At the end of the long sequence of rituals, the pilgrims return to Mecca and circle the Ka'aba once more. There, barbers cut three hairs from the pilgrims' heads. Many pilgrims thereafter also travel on to Medina to visit the tomb of the Prophet Muhammad in the mosque he founded in that city. Signs there warn the faithful against prostrating themselves before the tombs of the Prophet and his successors, for fear of betraying the central tenet of Islam: "There is no God but Allah. And Muhammad is his Prophet."

SPIRITUAL JOURNEYS

After their time spent in and around Mecca, most pilgrims swiftly make their way home again, laden with souvenirs, Medina dates, and bottles of Zamzam water. Many, perhaps most, are spiritually renewed and uplifted. Yet, as with any pilgrimage experience, individual reactions to the hajj may vary considerably. Some will be shocked that the great world of Islam is far more disparate than they realized, involving people from a variety of linguistic and cultural backgrounds. Some, such as the pilgrims from West Africa, will have traveled routes that have been followed for a thousand years, even consciously adopting older modes of travel, on camel or on foot, while others from new centers of Islam are less attached to the past. Theological differences within Islam also surface, notably the Shi'ite emphasis on the tombs of *imams*—Muslim leaders—and saints as sacred places to be visited and as conduits of grace equal to Mecca. Just as some within the Christian tradition react strongly against overritualizing, a strong thread within Islamic thought also seeks to diminish the importance of ritual observances.

Yet the evidence is inescapable. For the great majority of Muslims who have even a passing attachment to their religion, the hajj is a once-in-a-lifetime opportunity to connect with the great world of Islam and to build the Fifth Pillar that holds up that faith.

And hold fast together all of you to the faith of Allah and do not separate. Remember Allah's favor to you: how you were enemies and He made friendship in your hearts so that you became as brothers to each other by His grace. (Koran, Sura 3:103)

A pilgrimage obligatory for all believers is indeed a powerful force, emphasizing universal allegiance and practice in a religion that history has shown can readily be split by localized differences and difficulties.

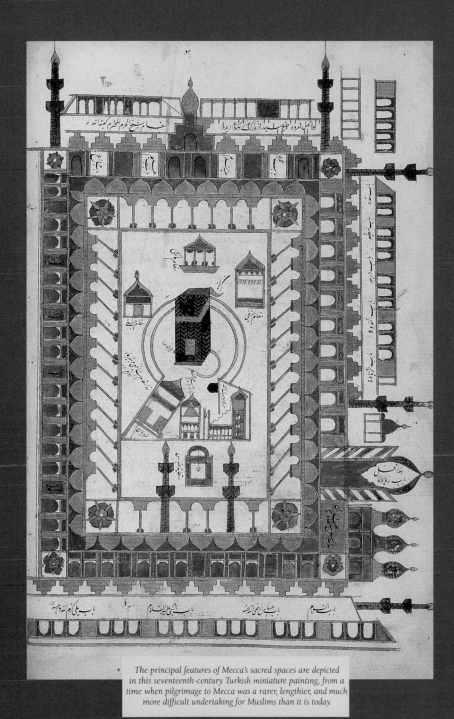

The principal features of Mecca's sacred spaces are depicted
in this seventeenth-century Turkish miniature painting, from a
time when pilgrimage to Mecca was a rarer, lengthier, and much
more difficult undertaking for Muslims than it is today.

A Tibetan Buddhist pilgrim clasps his hand in prayer on the arduous trek around Mount Kailas. His prayers join those of the adherents to three other religions who come to worship at the place many believe is the navel of the Earth.

JOURNEY THIRTEEN

Mount Kailas

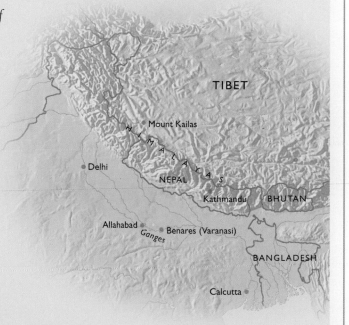

TO THE PILGRIMS of four separate religions, the center—the navel—of the Earth is a naturally formed rock pyramid 22,000 feet (6,700 meters) high located in a remote corner of Tibet. Mount Kailas rises in one of the highest, loneliest, and most desolate places on the planet.

ABOVE: As it spins, this Buddhist prayer wheel releases the thoughts and energies of a Tibetan pilgrim who will have undergone many hardships and privations to reach this holiest of pilgrim sites.

mid western Tibet's barren landscape is a luminous location, graced by great Buddhist monasteries perched on hilltops, crossed by biting winds and by bands of pilgrims: Buddhist, Hindu, Jain, and Bonpo. Here also four of India's great rivers rise—the Indus, Sutlej, Brahmaputra, and Karnali—a geographical fact that underwrites the mountain's mystical status.

AN ARDUOUS JOURNEY OF FAITH

The journey to Mount Kailas (also known as just Kailas or as Kailasa) is an arduous one, and since China's 1959 annexation of Tibet traveling to the sacred mountain has become even harder. Yet there are many who still make the great trek. The vision of the great universal mountain has spread throughout Asia, inspiring works of art and literature over the centuries. The great Buddhist stupa of Borobodur in Java, for example, is this mountain recreated in hewn stone.

Hindus in specially organized convoys cross the frozen mountain passes on the border with India to encircle the peak they regard to be the throne of Shiva and to bathe in the lake created from the mind of Brahma, two of the three great divinities of Hinduism. Buddhists journey to the Precious Snow Mountain that is at the heart of Asian views of the

universe, rooted in the seventh hell and piercing through the air to the highest heaven. For those pilgrims who are Jains, the mountain's great significance is that their primordial founder Rishabhanatha achieved spiritual liberation on its summit. To the Bonpo of remote southeastern Tibet, followers of Tibet's ancient pre-Buddhist religion, the peak is the Nine-Storey Swastika Mountain, the mystic soul of the world. A huge natural fissure on the mountain's north face is traditionally identified as a swastika, the ancient symbol of sun and rebirth.

TIBETAN BUDDHISM

Of all these religions, it is Buddhism that has the greatest impact. Tibetan Buddhism established a system of pilgrimage that is focused on sites of

BELOW LEFT: *The vast conical peak of Mount Kailas, seen on the right of the photograph, dominates the dry and wind-seared landscape just as it dominates the thoughts and hopes of the pilgrims who approach it via the stupas, prayer stations, and ritual pathways.*

BELOW: *The harsh winds that blow through this Himalayan landscape will also turn the prayer wheels that Buddhist pilgrims carry. This Tibetan woman is just setting out on a journey of spiritual endeavor to Mount Kailas that will crown a lifetime of prayer and devotion.*

The road to Mount Kailas that Buddhists, Bonpo, Jains, and Hindus all follow is long and hard whether traveled by vehicle or on foot. The mountain that is the pilgrims' destination is visible for a great distance, and it beckons them onward.

ABOVE: *A pilgrims' encampment on the high Himalayan plateau offers precious little protection from the effects of constant wind, biting cold, glare, and altitude.*

immensely complex and powerful symbolism. (In Zen, by contrast, a pilgrim's journey is undertaken for the sake of the spiritual state of mind in which the pilgrim travels.) Mount Kailas is the greatest of these sites, "the Mandala of the Highest Bliss." The sacred mountain is, in effect, mapped onto a sacred text, and to walk round it is to undertake a journey through a sacred space, one in which many gods have lived. Lama Anagarika Govinda, the most celebrated of modern guides to the sacred mountain,

wrote in *The Way of the White Clouds*, "He who performs the *Parikrama*, the ritual circumambulation of the holy mountain, with a perfectly devoted and concentrated mind goes through a full cycle of life and death."

The thirty-two-mile (forty-eight-kilometer) circuit of Mount Kailas is therefore a meditative as well as a physical journey. Milarepa, who was Tibet's beloved saint, roamed the Nepal–Tibet borderland almost a thousand years ago. Of his many songs, one in particular is of crucial significance to the story of Mount Kailas. It tells of how Milarepa met the Bonpo shaman Naro Bon Chun on the slopes of the mountain, and of how the shaman

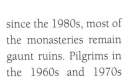

APPROACH TO THE
SACRED SITE

*He enters the red valley of
Amitabha in the mild light of the sinking
sun, goes through the portals
of death between the dark northern and
multicolored eastern valleys when
ascending the formidable Dolma-La,
the Pass of Tara, the Savioress—and he
descends, as a newborn being into the
green valley of Akshobya on the east of
Kailas, where the poet saint Milarepa
composed his hymns, and from where
the pilgrim again emerges into the
sunny, open plains of the south, assigned
to the Dhyani-Buddha Ratnasambhava,
whose color is that of gold.*

LAMA ANAGARIKA GOVINDA

lost all the contests of magic they held in order to determine which religion would hold sway over the sacred mountain. The sacred route still bears the scars, it is said, of the pair's titanic struggle.

Buddhism then prevailed for nearly a millennium until the new order imposed by the Chinese in 1959. Before the destruction following Chinese annexation and the Cultural Revolution, this area was the site of a number of important Buddhist monasteries. Although some have been rebuilt or repaired with the gradual thaw in external relations since the 1980s, most of the monasteries remain gaunt ruins. Pilgrims in the 1960s and 1970s had to perform their rituals illicitly, making their circumambulation in the course of a single night. In this way, despite the long years of repression, the holiness of the site was kept alive in the minds of many believers.

Where once trains of pack animals crossed the forbidding high plateau of western Tibet, and pilgrims walked for months, sometimes years, to their sacred destination, they now usually make the journey as passengers on freight trucks. The vestigial roads and the trucks are two of the novelties brought by the Chinese. The journey remains arduous and slow, for the distances to be covered are immense and the trucks commonly break down on the way. Young and old, men and women, monks, nuns, and ordinary Tibetans, all book their passage to the mountain. Supplies of butter-tea and the barley meal that are the staple foods of this region sustain the travelers as they make roadside and overnight stops, pitch their tents, and gather dried yak dung for their fires. The Tibetans have a proverb, "He who knows how to go about it can live comfortably even in hell," which seems entirely apposite to this particular road journey. The worldly and the divine coexist on the trek. It is an adventure as well as a time for reflection and prayer —but no one forgets the awe inspired in them by the sight of the mountain first glimpsed in the crystal-clear air.

Tarchen, the traditional pilgrims' resting place beneath the southern face of Mount Kailas, is a huddle of dun-covered buildings enlivened in the summer months by the constant arrival and departure of pilgrim trucks and traders. The circumambulation or *kora* begins here. A single circuit is supposed to erase the sins of a lifetime, but many do three kora, some thirteen, while the most devout of the seekers of Nirvana stay for a very long while and perform 108. To walk round Kailas in a single day may take twelve to seventeen hours, setting out well before dawn.

ABOVE: Believers both young and old undertake the arduous pilgrimage. Tibet was annexed by the People's Republic of China in 1959 and access to many sacred places was for a time severely restricted or forbidden, but the tradition remained defiantly unbroken.

THE PATHWAY

The path that the pilgrims follow starts at the destroyed castle, the hermitage of Ghu ya sgang pa, and continues in an easterly direction past monastic retreats to the Buddha Throne, where Buddha Sakyamuni recited the great holy text, the Lankavtara Sutra. Footprints of the Buddha and five hundred of his original followers exist at the site. More sacred footprints are visible at the mountains called the Golden Palace and the Black Palace of Shambala on each side of the Lha chu River. The route continues through the pass of sGrolma-La with its sacred pool below, and continues downhill

Prayer flags left by many of the pilgrims who have gone through this high Himalayan mountain pass are colourful and long-lasting testimony to the drawing power of Mount Kailas.

to the palaces of Tseringma and the Medicine Buddha, where many healing plants grow. There are statues of Hindu and Buddhist saints along the route to the last station on the circuit, the rGyangs grags Monastery. For Hindus it is not imperative to circumambulate the mountain; many are satisfied just to see Mount Kailas from Lake Manasarovar, considering this *darshan*—the experience of the presence of the numinous.

A much higher, inner kora circles the pyramidal peak that rises directly beneath Kailas. The path crosses a high pass beneath the south face of the mountain into a great natural amphitheater before doubling back again. To take this route a pilgrim must be specially blessed and have performed thirteen outer kora.

These pilgrims worship the unseen divine powers locked into this mountain region, confident in their belief that reality exists on multiple levels, some beyond their ordinary senses. Like the light mirages and the fantastical shapes created by the rock formations of the mountains, the visible reality on the circuit is, in the words of the Buddhist teacher Nagarjuna, "an illusion, a dream, a fairy city in the sky."

Along the route are stopping places where pilgrims prostrate themselves. Prayer-flags flutter in the mountain passes, propitiating the gods that in traditional Tibetan belief are the invisible guardians of the mountain routes. Pilgrims carry prayer-wheels that radiate sacred thoughts as they spin. Small cairns of stones mark the way and are expressions of the prayers of the devout, as are the strings of prayer-beads the pilgrims carry. Each step on the journey, each scramble up an unyielding large boulder, becomes itself a religious offering.

Bonpo pilgrims will have made a similarly arduous journey from their far-off homeland in southeastern Tibet before beginning their circuits, counterclockwise and so against the flow of Buddhist pilgrims. Hindus, often well-to-do people from the centers of Indian population who have to have obtained special government authorization to make their visit, trek through the mountains before reaching Tarchen by bus and setting out to make their circuits on yak, horseback, or on foot.

KAILAS' MIRROR

The monasteries often had two focuses: the great mountain, and its counterpart, the vast Lake Manasarovar in which Buddha's mother, Queen Maya, was said to have bathed in a dream to purify herself before the Buddha was conceived. The great lake below the mountain is the mirror reflecting the glory of the mystic mountain. The highest sweetwater lake in the world, at a height of 14,950 feet (4,558 meters), the lake has been venerated as a holy place for at least three thousand years.

To Tibetan Buddhists, Manasarovar is the precious mother as Kailas is the father. If the mountain is the sun, the lake is its moon, a shifting and fluid turquoise mirror meant for contemplation. Hindus have venerated the divine lake for thousands of years. Its great size—fifteen miles (twenty-two kilometers) wide and thirty miles (fifty kilometers) around—and its rocky shore make a circuit of the lake difficult. While the Buddhists contemplate it and may drink from it, for Hindu pilgrims it is important to bathe in the lake's icy waters.

A LIVING TRADITION

Despite the attempts of the Chinese authorities to repress and remove the spirit of the religion, Buddhism remains a living tradition in Tibet. Since 1980, the Chinese authorities have embarked on a limited program of accommodation. Monasteries and sacred sites that were destroyed have sometimes been rebuilt, and pilgrims and tourists have been allowed back into the region. The numbers are necessarily limited, since the arduous nature of the journey will put off all but the most dedicated seekers of enlightenment. Yet every year thousands, and sometimes tens of thousands, whether on foot or now in the four-wheel drive vehicles of international spiritual tourism, brave the physical difficulties of getting there to trek around the base of the sacred mountain and to bathe in Manasarovar. As Kailas begins to appear on the most hardy tourist itineraries, something of its uniqueness may be lost.

Anyone with enough determination can get to Mount Kailas. It may seem merely superstitious to nonbelievers, but the tracing of a vast circle, itself one of the great cosmological devices, is an active form of meditation. The mind is centered on the axis and the individual is subsumed into the cosmic pattern. He or she is no longer separate but part of the whole.

A pilgrim to Mount Kailas must be open to the transformation that both the journey and the destination can—and should—bring. In a true pilgrimage, the journey lifts the traveler out of the everyday self into a realm beyond the ego. There is particular spiritual merit in walking around the mountain for the devout in all four religions that venerate it. The pilgrims will attain spiritual purification and the awakening of their inner being.

To those who behold it, the pilgrims' response to Mount Kailas is emotionally moving. Yet beneath such emotions is a deeper truth, for a pilgrim's faith *can* move mountains, lifting a peak into the realm of the divine and creating of it a symbol for the unifying center of all creation.

BELOW: The actions of snow and ice have shaped the Tibetan Himalayas, providing the ancient bedrock of many systems of belief.

Women from Mahararashtra rest on the pilgrimage route to Vithoba's temple at Pandharpur. The act of getting there, for Indian pilgrims like these, is as important as the destination.

JOURNEY FOURTEEN

Pandharpur

ONE OF THE MOST FAMOUS *Hindu pilgrimages occurs every year in the west Indian state of Maharashtra, on the sacred routes to and around the small town of Pandharpur. To get the most from the experience, these pilgrims must follow an ancient prescribed set of stations along a route hundreds of miles long to the temple of the deity Vithoba (one of the forms taken by the great Lord Krishna). This is therefore one of those pilgrimages in which the journey to the site is just as important as the site itself.*

LEFT: *Richly decorated floats and colorful processions are integral to the celebration and worship of India's many deities. At Pandharpur, pride of place is taken by the Lord Krishna himself as Vithoba.*

En route to Pandharpur, pilgrims may find that the journey becomes a spiritualized experience in itself. Although some pilgrimages are made for very specific purposes—to seek healing or divine intervention, in atonement, or to reduce the rigors of the afterlife—others are undertaken out of the sheer joy of rendering devotion and showing respect for traditional values. That seems to be what impels the annual pilgrimages centered on Pandharpur.

THE JOYS OF OFFERING

Every year two pilgrimages, one large and one small, involve this ordinarily tiny town some 200 miles (320 kilometers) southeast of Mumbai (Bombay). The larger pilgrimage culminates there on the banks of the River Bhima on the "bright eleventh" day of the lunar month of Asadha, which currently falls in June–July. Four-and-a-half months later, pilgrims follow the route in reverse to reach the temple town of Alandi. On the banks of the Indrayani River, Alandi is at the western end of the long traditional route that connects these two places sacred to Krishna in his embodiment as Vithoba.

VITHOBA AND PUNDALIK

An ancient story explains the presence of Vithoba at both Pandharpur and Alandi and how the early holy men who journeyed there instituted pilgrimage to the two towns.

Once, it seems, the mature Krishna—who embodied all the younger Krishnas beloved of Hindus—was revisited by the love of his youth, Radha. Leaving his wife Rukmini, Krishna searched for Radha in the forests of Maharashtra, but to no avail. He did, however, find a young man, Pundalik, on the banks of the Bhima. At first

ABOVE: Making a joyful noise, pilgrims on the road follow the route that Pundalik is said to have taken to a hut on the banks of the River Bhima, where he was to encounter the Lord Krishna.

Pundalik was intent on caring for his elderly father and took no notice of the great Lord Krishna. But Krishna sent out so much radiant energy that eventually Pundalik could ignore the god no longer. Displaying his filial piety, he threw a brick over his shoulder for Krishna to stand upon off the wet ground. Profoundly impressed, Krishna gave up his search for Radha, called Rukmini to his side, and stayed there. And there the holy pair still stand as temple statues, portrayed perched on the brick in front of Pundalik's hut. Thereafter, this new form of Krishna was called Vithoba.

Since the god is fixed, it is his devotees who must move. Pundalik himself, who had been a willful and headstrong young man, had abandoned his other plans in order to return to care for his elderly parents. His journey from Alandi is commemorated in the pilgrimage to Pandharpur. From the thirteenth century onward, various holy men have made their way to worship this new form of Krishna as Vithoba. Their journeys have been added to the overall scheme of the pilgrimage, and an intricate web of pilgrim paths connects

*The bright colors of the figures of the gods and the raw
music accompanying the processional floats are integral
to the celebrations at Pandharpur.*

twenty-eight places in the hinterland of Pandharpur with the central temple at the site of Pundalik's hut on the banks of the Bhima. Although most pilgrims come from the central plains of Maharashtra, others come from the fishing communities on the coast and from the pastoral settlements in the hills of the interior. They call their destination "Paradise on Earth."

TOWARD THE BRIGHT ELEVENTH

In the latter days of the lunar month of Jyestha, Vithoba's devotees begin their journey to his principal city of Pandharpur. They will enter the city in one great procession on the *sukla ekadasi* (bright eleventh) of the lunar month of Asadha. Special buses make the trip, but the majority walk at least some of the way. As many as ten thousand people will have come to Pandharpur on foot, mainly in the thirty or more organized parties that make up the core of the pilgrimage. Each of these parties, called *palkhis* (and their subdivisions in the larger groups, *dindis*), has its own prescribed route. The palkhi from Alandi, the largest and most tightly organized, has a rigid timetable, following the path via Poona (Pune), Jejuri, Lonand, Phaltan, Natepute, Velapur and finally Wakri just outside Pandharpur; the length of stay in each place is determined by the moon's phases that year. The strict organization includes provisions, trucks, and set fees. Other parties from smaller places are much less carefully controlled, having but a starting and a finishing date and a only a general sense of the direction to be followed.

Nowadays some pilgrim groups are coordinated through the Internet as much as by traditional oral forms of communication: employees of the national airline, Air India, have their own palkhi, for example. In 1999, the staff were told what to expect:

There will be a rush to take a holy bath in the River Chandrabhaga. The sky will be filled with the chants of 'Dyanoba Mauli Tukaram' and 'Jai Hari Vitthal'. Varkaris with banners, pendants and accompanying musical instruments and [the] singing of Hari path will participate in [the] yearly pilgrimage with [their] heart and soul. Devotees [wrapped up] in their own families [may] have a [secret] wish to participate in the annual Dindi and walk at least a few steps with fellow pilgrims. While fulfilling the needs of such devotees, Air India Employees will celebrate Dhakli Dindi [for the] fourth year in succession.

Nominated members of each palkhi carry silver replicas of the feet of one of the cult's saints, those early holy men. The feet, borne in state on a palanquin, commemorate the saints' own pilgrimage centuries before. These pilgrims are thus directly connected with their forebears. Other rituals commemorate the original pilgrimages—a riderless horse followed by a ridden horse leads the procession, and prayers are said at traditional way stations en route. Finally, when everybody has assembled at Wakri, greetings given and received, and a ritual meal eaten, the throng wends its way into Pandharpur and the temple of Vitobha, standing on his brick.

The noisy and joyous procession through the town to the temple takes all day. Many pilgrims stand patiently in line through the night for the few seconds they each have to touch Vithoba's feet and receive in return his divine power. If they are lucky, the moonlight is bright; but often by this time of year the monsoon has arrived, the River Bhima is in spate and bathing is ill advised. The coastal fishermen, who have brought their boats as part of the ritual, ferry pilgrims to the traditional site of Pundalik's filial devotions. In the monsoon, his temple may be half-submerged, and pilgrims have to crouch down in the boats to see into the top half of the shrine doorway.

ABOVE: *Pilgrims take their nourishment as they wait patiently for the chance to glimpse inside the temple and touch the effigy of Vithoba, standing proudly on the brick that Pundalik had thrown away.*

AFTER THE BRIGHT ELEVENTH

The procession over, their offerings complete, and the blessing of Vithoba bestowed upon them, the pilgrims then swiftly disperse and make their way home again, to await the next year's pilgrimage. A minority of them will make the second pilgrimage to Alandi, at the other end of this principal route, starting out sixteen weeks later on the "bright eleventh" of the lunar month of Kartika and taking two weeks to complete the journey temple so that they arrive on the "dark eleventh". By doing this they honour Jnaneshwar, one of the original holy men and the cult's premier saint. Those who promise always to make this double pilgrimage, for as long as they are able, are known as Varkaris. Specially blessed, some may eventually become holy men and renounce the material world, throwing themselves wholeheartedly into the ritual round and the pilgrimage of life that is one of the great features of Hinduism.

Beneath the great baldacchino and under the soaring dome of St. Peter's Basilica, the Pope, Christ's vicar on earth, celebrates the mass for Christ's nativity on earth for the clergy, the pilgrims, and those local to Rome.

Rome

THE EXPRESSION *"the road to Rome"* has had two meanings in the past couple of centuries: not only does it refer to the literal route to the city via towns, mountain passes, and river plains; it also refers to the religious conversion of those who seek admission to or reconciliation with the Roman Catholic Church.

ALPS

Aosta

Vercelli
Pavia
Piacenza
Parma

MONACO

Lucca
Siena

CORSICA

Viterbo

Rome

ITALY

SARDINIA

MEDITERRANEAN SEA

SICILY

APPENINES

BELOW: The great baroque frontage of St. Peter's Basilica, with its entrance doorways open, including the Holy Door that is only opened for pilgrims in Jubilee years.

For early-twentieth-century essayist and tragicomic poet Hilaire Belloc, the two roads to Rome were one and the same. Like many before him, he found that the physical route and the metaphorical route coincided.

ETERNAL CITY, PAPAL CITY

Rome was the city that conquered most of the ancient Western world. Its empire stretched from Scotland to Africa, Portugal to Romania. The Catholic Church, based in Rome, is lineally descended from the early followers of Jesus Christ; its spiritual leader, the Pope, can claim his authority stems directly from St. Peter, the apostle to whom Christ himself gave primacy as spokesman. It matters little that in the course of two millennia there have been popes and antipopes, warrior popes and syphilitic popes, saintly popes and scholarly popes, exiled popes and murdered popes. For all that time, Rome has been revered as the site where Peter and his proselytizing fellow disciple

ABOVE: *This grand and sweeping panorama with St. Peter's Basilica in the foreground, was the sight that pilgrims were privileged to see after their long and gruelling journey across the Alps and through Italy.*

Paul were executed in AD 64 and 65 for their revolutionary faith and where they were buried. Other early Christians joined them in a martyr's death.

When the Emperor Constantine officially converted the Roman Empire to the new Christian faith in 313, the bishop of Rome was leader of the growing religion, and he has remained so. Schisms with other traditions in the East and the reaction that led to the foundation of the Protestant Churches in the sixteenth century have merely dented the Roman Catholic Church's supremacy.

ROADS TO ROME

The expression "All roads lead to Rome" may have been coined in the days of empire, but it remained equally true for medieval Christian pilgrimages. In Italy, the *Via Romea*—otherwise known as the *Via Francigena* (the Frankish Way)—was the road from the north that pilgrims have traveled since the Dark Ages. Crossing the Alps by the Great St. Bernard Pass, pilgrims followed a set of paths by way of Aosta, Vercelli, Pavia, Piacenza, and Parma, taking various routes across the Apennines to

The road fell into a hollow where soldiers were manoeuvring. Even these could not arrest an attention that was fixed upon the approaching revelation. It was now warm day, trees of great height stood shading the sun, the place had taken on an appearance of wealth and care. The mist had gone before I reached the summit of the rise.

There, from the summit, between the high villa walls on either side – at my very feet I saw the City.

Hilaire Belloc, *The Path to Rome* (1902)

since Christ said to Peter: "And I shall give to you the keys of the kingdom of Heaven." Unlike the road to Santiago de Compostela (see chapter eighteen), there are few vestiges now of that ancient route: most pilgrims' hostels have vanished without trace or are forgotten half-ruins. Those at Altopascio, near Lucca, and Poggibonsi, near Siena, are rare survivors. Some pilgrims still walk or ride along the ancient route, but nothing is like the traffic on the Way of St. James en route to Santiago de Compostela in northern Spain where pilgrimage has been so successfully revived. Yet the churches and cathedrals along the way are still potent reminders of the old road to Rome: the great baptistery at Parma was decorated as a pilgrim sanctuary, and the sculptures on many churches incorporate the themes of sin and redemption and the symbol of the labyrinth, the pilgrim's journey on earth.

At journey's end, the medieval pilgrim road did not enter Rome directly but took a route from the south on what is now the Via Trionfale. That gave the first sight of the city in a splendid panorama (see illustration, pp136–37).

ABOVE: *Below the walls of Rome's Castel Sant'Angelo, the Pope blesses St. Ursula and her band of eleven thousand virgins who, according to legend, went on pilgrimage and suffered cruel martyrs' deaths.*

Lucca, Siena, and Viterbo, and so from there to Rome. The meaning of the word *romeo*, in fact, is "a pilgrim bound for Rome." British pilgrims would have gathered at Canterbury, crossed from Dover, and passed through Rheims, Besançon, and Lausanne. This was the route that Sigeric took in 994, recorded in one of the earliest descriptions of the journey to Rome, in order to be invested as archbishop of Canterbury. (He took fifty days each way, and spent only three days in Rome.)

As modern pilgrims to Lourdes carry back plastic bottles of spring water, so pilgrims to Rome brought back crossed keys, the symbol of St. Peter,

THE FIRST PILGRIMS

Some of the earliest evidence of Christian pilgrimage comes from Rome. Graffiti on the walls of the catacombs indicate the religious visits of pilgrims as early as the third century. A century later, once Christianity became the official religion of the Empire, the trickle of visits swelled to a flood. In considerable crossover with older, pre-Christian observances, pilgrims might have eaten the *agape* ("loving meal") in the company of the dead or sleep in a basilica hoping for a disease to be cured.

In AD 330, Constantinople replaced Rome as the imperial city. Yet even afterward, Rome remained the holy city. The residing pope *Pontifex Maximus,* the supreme pontiff or "bridge-builder"—a title taken from the rulers of ancient and imperial Rome —dispensed justice throughout the Christian world. Pilgrims did not come to see the pope, however, but to revere the tombs of the martyrs, the brave men and women who had died for their faith in the early and difficult days of Christianity. Nowadays, we have lost the sense early Christians must have had of the near miracle it was that a small, dissident religious group could grow into the vast Church it was becoming. By the time the imperial capital had transferred to Constantinople, pilgrims were hoping for miracles from the relics of saints—and relics were certainly not hard to find in Rome. Gradually those relics were brought out of the catacombs and transferred into individual churches and basilicas, the seventh- and eighth-century forerunners of the churches dotted around Rome today. The network of roads and pilgrim hostels was already taking shape in the sixth century helping to speed travelers, while in Rome national hostels or *scholae* were set up to provide accommodations for those from a particular country, the first of them the *Schola Saxonum* for the English in 717, founded by Ina, King of Wessex.

Saints' bones were not all there were to venerate. Through gift and conquest, Rome acquired a vast array of sacred artifacts, from fragments of the True Cross to the stone tablets Moses brought down bearing the Ten Commandments. Two of the greatest attractions were the *Sudarium*—the cloth that bore the image of Jesus' face after St. Veronica used it to wipe his brow on the way to his execution—and the *Scala Santa* (Holy Staircase) at the Basilica of St. John Lateran. This is the staircase transported from what was believed to be Pontius Pilate's house in Jerusalem, up which Christ would have walked on the eve of his Crucifixion. Pilgrims do not walk up this holy staircase but ascend it on their knees.

ABOVE: Austrian pilgrims gather for a torchlight service in the Catacombs, to remember the ordeal of early Christians martyred in Rome for their faith, and to commit themselves to Christian Rome.

Even the Old Testament was cited to bolster the city's special claims—one twelfth-century guidebook asserted that Rome had been founded, not by Romulus and Remus, but by Noah on his travels.

THE SEVEN CHURCHES

When indulgences—remission of time in purgatory in "exchange" for deeds and observances—were coming into vogue in the eleventh and twelfth centuries, successive popes offered special favors to those who came on pilgrimage to Rome. A specific circuit on the edge of the ancient city was adopted

ABOVE: *The vast spaces of St. Peter's Basilica dwarf the pilgrims who come to seek the roots of their faith, to glimpse their spiritual leader, and to participate in the ancient ceremonial of Roman Catholicism.*

to take in the seven principal churches: St. Peter's, St. Paul's Outside the Walls, Santa Maria Maggiore, St. John Lateran, Santa Croce, San Lorenzo, and San Sebastiano. Modern-day pilgrims continue to follow this circuit. Many relics exist in these churches still, and San Sabastiano provides access to the most important set of catacombs, the subterranean cemeteries that were such a focus of early Christian life in Rome. St. Paul's bones may have been stolen by Arab invaders in 846, who looted his sarcophagus in the search for gold and silver, but the heads of both St. Peter and St. Paul are housed, it is said, in a magnificent reliquary on the high altar in St. John Lateran.

St. Peter himself is officially stated to have been buried beneath what has since become the greatest Christian church in the world, St. Peter's Basilica in the Vatican. When Pope Pius XII ordered the lowering of the floors of the sacred grottoes beneath the basilica to prepare a tomb for his predecessor, Pius XI, in 1939, revealed was not only Constantine's basilica floor but also an ancient tomb shrine located directly beneath the high altar. During the subsequent wartime years an ancient cemetery was uncovered containing tombs both pagan and Christian. Eventually, nearly forty years after the first discovery, the bones of an elderly man found beside the principal subterranean shrine were proclaimed to be those of St. Peter. After more than a thousand years of being hidden, the ancient necropolis is again one of the principal sights a pilgrim would hope to view, although access is difficult and expensive to arrange.

Constantine began to build his richly decorated basilica over the apostle's tomb in 324. Its campanile (bell tower) was surmounted by a golden cockerel that would, everybody said, crow when the end of the world had arrived. A thousand years later this church was falling to pieces, and the cockerel fell before the world has. Under Pope Julius II, the architects Bramante, Raphael, Peruzzi, Sangallo—and eventually, in 1546—Michelangelo were commissioned to build a replacement church. Each meddled in his predecessors' designs, and later architects interfered with Michelangelo's grand gestures. In 1626 the church was consecrated, a glorious exercise in architectural compromise, now filled with masterpieces of religious art.

At the enormous northeastern crossing pier sits the bronze statue of St. Peter, possibly fifth-century in date. The extended foot of the apostle has been worn away by the kisses of pilgrims over the centuries. Above the high altar soars the world's largest dome (by volume). At the entrance portico, the right-most of the great bronze doors is the Holy Door (the present one was designed in 1950), which is opened only in jubilee years.

ABOVE: A young friar says his daily office with the dome of St. Peter's as his inspiring backdrop. Rome has always attracted scholars and those with religious vocations among its many pilgrims.

JUBILEE

Jubilee ultimately derives from a Hebrew word that means "ram's horn"—the instrument that was blown like a trumpet to proclaim the beginning of the great celebrations held every fifty years in Israel. In a jubilee year, slaves were freed, debts were forgiven, and disputed property was amicably allocated. Christians adopted the idea of jubilee during the Crusades when Jerusalem was temporarily liberated from Muslim rule, and in 1300 the first great jubilee was held in Rome. Huge bands of pilgrims thereupon descended on the city. The notion of the jubilee seems to have come from a great whispering campaign—it certainly appears not to have been officially formulated—but the papacy swiftly grasped the spiritual and commer-

cial opportunities it offered. Among those first jubilee pilgrims was Dante Alighieri, and his *Divina Commedia* ("Divine Comedy") opens in Rome on Good Friday 1300. Jubilees have taken place (with a few exceptions owing to difficult political circumstances) every fifty years since.

The years 1500 and 2000 were, for obvious calendrical reasons, times of special celebration. On Christmas Eve 1999 the Pope followed tradition and ceremonially opened the Holy Door as the signal that the millennial jubilee had begun. At the Feast of the Epiphany (January 6) 2001, it was walled up again. Some twenty million pilgrims thronged Rome in the course of that single year.

TO THE CITY AND THE WORLD

The vast St. Peter's Square in front of the Basilica and the Vatican palace—its dimensions match those of the Colosseum—can easily contain a quarter of a million people. On occasions it holds many more. This is where the majority of today's pilgrims to Rome congregate. They come especially to hear Mass said by the Holy Father in the open air on a Sunday and the great feast days, or to receive his blessing given from the palace window. The devout and the curious, nuns and priests, sturdy backpackers and the wheelchair-bound throng the square. On Easter Day the papal blessing *Urbi et Orbi*—to the city and to the world—is televised around the globe. Pilgrims with advance tickets attend a papal audience on a Wednesday morning, either outside in the piazza from May to September or inside the Vatican, the papal state, in the Nervi Auditorium. Some happy pilgrims will unfurl banners proclaiming where their particular group has come from, whether Cincinnati, Cuzco, Coímbra, or Cork.

While the cult of saints and relics may have withered, Rome's attractions of antiquity and art treasures, and above all the papacy, have ensured its status as the single most important destination for pilgrimage in the Christian world. In Rome, as is true at many sacred sites, the distinction between visitor, tourist, and pilgrim is often blurred—but the true pilgrims know who they are.

RIGHT: Crowds gather in St. Peter's Square to hear St. Peter's earthly successor Pope Paul VI say Mass, watched over by the figures of St. Peter and the other apostles placed there by Michelangelo.

*St. Anne is the Mother of God to whom both the French
and the French Canadians have long been devoted. Her
shrine in Quebec has drawn French-speaking
Native Americans for over three centuries.*

JOURNEY SIXTEEN

Ste. Anne de Beaupré

THEY COME HERE BY THE BUSLOAD—elderly blue-rinsed grand-mères *from the environs of Montreal, schoolchildren from the walled defenses of Quebec City, and French speakers from neighboring Ontario or upper New York state. Native Americans arrive in their battered pickups. Thick-jacketed skiers approach gingerly in rented four-wheel drives.*

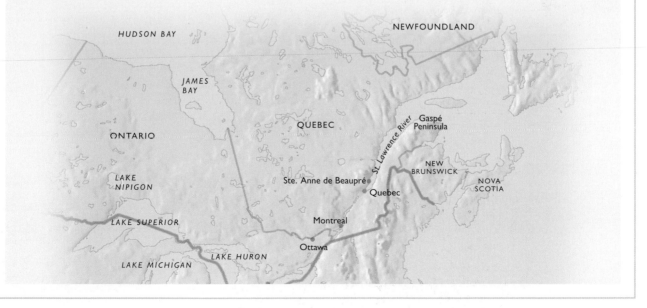

The Roman Catholic shrine of St. Anne is the oldest in North America. It also stands apart from most of the continent because of language. In Quebec, French is jealously and zealously guarded. While Our Lady at Czestochowa has been an enduring symbol of Polish nationhood (in Europe and in North America) over the centuries, her mother, St. Anne, has long been an emblem that helps set French Canada apart from the anglophone world.

ST. ANNE COMES TO NORTH AMERICA

The French who first settled Canada came mainly from Brittany and Normandy. Always before setting off on the water, these fishermen would pay their respects at a local shrine, usually dedicated either to Our Lady or to St. Anne. In church after church in northwestern France, Jesus' mother-to-be is shown being given the rudiments of an education. In some tableaux, Mary is a naughty schoolgirl, her mother a taskmistress; in others, Mary is a willing pupil. These old devotions were carried in the seventeenth century to the new and dangerous land of Canada where, like the language the settlers spoke, they took root. In francophone Catholic Canada—principally Quebec but also its neighboring provinces—and states south of what is now the U.S. border, there are many shrines and altars dedicated to the greatest *grand-mère* of them all.

At some point around 1649, a group of sailors sought refuge from a storm on a small cape on the northern shore of the mighty St. Lawrence River, fewer than twenty miles (thirty-six kilometers) east of Quebec City. It was a quiet spot with a lovely meadow, the *beau pré*, and there the seafarers set up a tiny chapel to St. Anne just as they might have done back in Brittany. A new church was marked out in 1658, and during its foundation ceremony St. Anne was said to have worked her first miracle,

curing a local inhabitant crippled with rheumatism. This wooden chapel was never actually completed—because the vast river ice floes of spring swept it away—so a new one was built slightly farther downstream on higher ground. Completed in 1669, it contained a statue, brought from France, of St. Anne and her infant daughter Mary. A stream of pilgrims soon attested to the miracle-working powers of this statue, enthroned inside the church, once St. Anne's intercession had been invoked.

The statue has survived seemingly against all odds, inasmuch as the church has been demolished, rebuilt, burned down, and reedified many times since. The first stone church was begun in 1676, and was replaced by a great basilica two hundred years later. It and its successor both burned to the ground, in 1922 and again in 1926, before the present prodigious basilica was built. Apart from the statue and one or two relics of the saint, in particular a bone from her wrist that was brought from France in 1892 (with all the necessary documentation on its authenticity), little of antiquity is left. Yet enough remains to have attracted pilgrims for three and a half centuries. In around 1900 the shrine was at the height of its fame, and the international Eucharistic Congress, held in Montreal in 1910, brought it world recognition. A description from that time recorded, "The rear pillars of the church are lost in a rising phalanx of canes and crutches. The blind leave their black glasses behind them, grateful clients send *ex voto* tablets and rich rings, bracelets and necklets of gold and jewels for favors received."

SETTLING WITH THE NATIVE AMERICANS

From the beginning, the missionary activities of the Jesuits and Franciscans among the natives brought many converts to the several local shrines. The principal Native American tribe of the area was the

Pilgrims gather in front of the basilica, the sixth church on this site, to honor Anne and to invoke her healing powers. The crowds gather on her feast day in July and on Mary's feasts, and many pilgrims will also brave the winter snows.

Penitent pilgrims of a century ago ascend the Scala Santa
or Holy Staircase, a copy of the original in Rome.
A sequence of such sacred places reminds Quebec's
Catholics that they are tied to a world religion.

Micmac. Missionary activity dates from the very earliest days of French colonization, since the great explorer Samuel de Champlain brought 1,600 priests from his native town of Brouage. In 1610 Membertou, high chief of the Micmacs, was baptized by a missionary priest, and the rest of his people soon followed suit. Taught by the French priests to regard St. Anne as their as well as Jesus' grandmother, the Micmacs took the idea to heart and customarily dedicated all their churches and mission stations to her. Shrines and pilgrimages to St. Anne appear throughout this quarter of North America, even on one of the small islands in the middle of Lake Champlain (named after the great explorer) that divides the states of Vermont and New York.

The last great sea battle in the long struggle between France and Britain for control of Canada was fought in 1760 off Restigouche, on the coastal peninsula of Gaspé (south of the St. Lawrence River and facing the British territory of New Brunswick). That remains the center of the Micmac reservation to this day. The shrine of Sainte Anne-de-Micmacs continues to thrive there, although the British ensured that French priests were deported and English-speaking settlers occupied the land. The Micmacs and other native people were—and still are—assiduous visitors to the shrine at Beaupré. Records from the late seventeenth century indicate groups of up to eighteen birch-bark canoes being paddled along the mighty St. Lawrence River. The Christian Native Americans ran their light craft ashore and walked in silence and with dignity to the shrine, where their prayers and songs in their own language mingled with the Latin words of the Catholic Mass. Today there are trailer parks and overnight camping grounds for the tourists and for the many Native Americans who continue to come to the shrine—but by different means of transportation.

CURES AND CURÉS

Other than the great basilica at the shrine of St. Anne, there are also chapels built around a facsimile of the *Scala Santa* (Holy Staircase) in Rome. (Originally brought to Rome from Jerusalem by Constantine's mother, St. Helena, this staircase is believed to be the one Christ ascended in Pontius Pilate's palace before his Crucifixion.) Sainte Anne's pilgrims are not obliged to go up on their knees, although some do so. Life-size Stations of the Cross in bronze run along the edge of the hill behind the shrine. The healing waters of the Fountain of St. Anne are thronged with pilgrims seeking relief for their own ailments or dipping diseased and disabled relatives and friends into its waters. The roll-call of cures effected here is impressive, although—as at Lourdes—the Roman Catholic Church over the last century has become much harder to satisfy on the question of the authenticity of miracles. In the hospital at the end of the plaza near the church, some patients are cared for by what might well now be considered more conventional methods, within earshot of the bells of the basilica.

After many years of limited attention following the shrine's origins in the seventeenth century, interest revived in the 1870s. The cause can be traced not only to the worldwide resurgence of Roman Catholicism incorporating the strong attitude adopted by Pope Pius IX, the promulgator of the doctrine of papal infallibility, but also to the example set by the great shrine of the French-speaking world, Lourdes. Here Quebec had its own healing shrine, of far greater antiquity, and with its own roster of miraculous cures. The strong nationalist appeal of Lourdes could not fail to be heard in the French territory that was an integral part of the British Empire and Dominions.

Now more than a million pilgrims a year come to the shrine; in some years numbers exceed two million. They hear Mass and say the rosary prayers,

Her finger raised in benediction and in maternal admonition, St. Anne carries the infant Mary. The holy statue that was brought from France to the shores of the St. Lawrence in 1669 has conferred blessings and cures on the faithful ever since.

ABOVE: *The pilgrims' goal, especially at the July feast of St. Anne or any of Our Lady's feastdays, is to hear Mass at the shrine and to feel part of a 350-year-long tradition of prayer, hope, and French solidarity.*

they attend Benediction, they follow the stations of the cross indoors or outdoors depending on the weather, and they ascend the Holy Stair. The feast day of St. Anne on July 25 and the feasts of Our Lady attract the greatest numbers of pilgrims.

Sainte Anne de Beaupré is one of the three leading Catholic pilgrim sites not only in Quebec but in the whole of North America. Given the vast distances that many pilgrims have to cover, Sainte Anne de Beaupré is on a recognizable spiritual circuit. Budget motels line the road from Quebec City to Beaupré. Pilgrims from the United States and the eastern and western provinces of Canada take in a sequence of religious sites on their bus tours, such as the Martyrs' shrine in Ontario, the Fátima shrine in New York state, and the other main Quebec shrines at Beauvoir, Montreal, Trois Rivières, and Sillery. The scenery close to Beaupré offer other opportunities for contemplation.

There is also dual seasonality at Sainte Anne de Beaupré. Pilgrims come in the summer, between May and October, and again in the freezing winter months. That reason is not the mortification of the flesh. The premier ski resort of Mont Sainte Anne is four miles (seven kilometers) to the north of the shrine, and winter vacationers often combine the profane with the sacred. The pilgrim cult of St. Anne is part of the essence of Quebecois society.

The golden image of Moroni, the angel who delivered the Book of Mormon to Joseph Smith, tops the tallest of the soaring solid granite spires of the Mormon Tabernacle that stands in the heart of Salt Lake City.

Salt Lake City

BEFORE HE LED THE MORMON PIONEERS westward in 1847, Brigham Young expressed his yearning for "a land that nobody else wanted" where he and his followers would be free to practice according to their religious beliefs. He found it in Utah. There the members of the Church of Jesus Christ of Latter-day Saints, which he had helped found, would find sanctuary from persecution. There they would build what they believed was the true Church of Christ. Even today, Utah remains a place apart, not quite like the rest of the country.

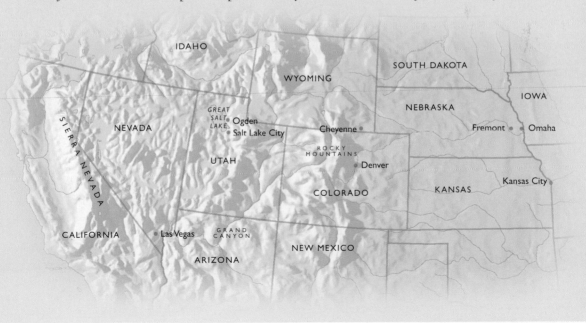

Those living in Salt Lake City are ever-mindful of how it was founded by determined and strong pioneers who came in search of isolation and endured incredible hardships for the simple privilege of being left alone. Setting themselves apart from mainstream Christian society and openly practicing polygamy, the early Mormons suffered for their religion. Since missionary activities are an essential part of Mormonism, Salt Lake City, the city that Brigham Young founded as the capital of Utah, has become the center of an international Church. It contains the buildings, the shrines, and the memories of separateness that a significant number of the four million Mormons journey to see.

UNPROMISING LAND

Utah was hardly a hospitable opportunity for new settlers in the mid-nineteenth century. The western explorer John Frémont had identified a land that had fertile pockets but was isolated from the rest of humankind, in a region that was otherwise deserted, arid, and desolate. The Great Basin is a region of dry prehistoric lake beds, rugged peaks and valleys, and interminable salt flats. The water

BELOW: A panoramic view of Salt Lake City as it is today. To Brigham Young this seemingly inhospitable tract of country was the perfect setting for establishing the Mormons' new homeland.

courses have no outlets to sea and simply evaporate. Two major mountain ranges cut the area off from the rest of the world, through which in July 1847 the original Mormon pilgrims were to pass before descending to the Salt Lake Valley below. The story goes that at the time Brigham Young was so sick from Colorado tick fever that he had to be assisted from his wagon to survey the valley. The words he spoke as he looked over the scene of barren desolation are known to all Mormons: "It is enough. This is the right place. Drive on."

A few other intrepid white travelers had preceded him, in search of furs or adventure. Young bought out the only existing white settlement, a tiny collection of huts that had been erected only the year before his pioneers set forth. His plans encompassed a huge area of southwestern North America, as far as California and including most of Nevada and Arizona. The empire was to be called *Deseret*, a word from the Book of Mormon that meant—with seeming incongruity—"honey-bees." Yet the land proved more hospitable than it appeared. Within a few days of reaching the Great Salt Lake, the first Mormon settlers were plowing the land and building roads to bring out timber, a fort to protect themselves against Indian incursions, and a leafy bower for Sunday worship. On July 28, Young marked with his cane the position on which the Mormon temple would be built; the city plan was set out according to the "Plan of the City of Zion," previously drawn up by Joseph Smith, Mormonism's founder, in 1833. Streets 132 feet (forty meters) wide ran north, south, east, and west, with the Temple Square at the center. Land plots were to be parceled out according to need.

The new Mormon empire had begun. The only difficulty was that technically this land was still owned by Mexico, although under the Treaty of Guadalupe Hidalgo it became American soil in 1848—the year after Young set out. Moreover, the

few Native Americans in the area proved not to present a problem, because the Ute people did not have permanent settlements there. And in any case, Young's attitude was that it was "better to feed them than to fight them," so relations were good. Within a few short years, great numbers of Mormons made the difficult trek westward. By 1855, the original four hundred settlers had grown to sixty thousand.

The United States Congress had refused the Mormons' petition in 1849 to make this vast area a state, but gave Utah territorial status with Young as

BELOW: Memories of the heroic pioneer struggle and the hardships undergone by the early Mormon families who came here are kept alive by the stream of pilgrims to Salt Lake City.

ABOVE: Museums and re-creations of pioneer existence, as well as marked trails that the early Mormons followed from the east, maintain the sense of their achievement against many odds.

its governor. However, the federal government in Washington, D.C., grew ever more suspicious of the Mormons, especially when the Church made its open declaration in favor of polygamy and some of the more militant Mormons were implicated in violence against their enemies. By 1857 suspicion was being translated into federal military action.

Armed standoffs continued for ten years, but were never translated into direct action or bloodshed. The major change came in 1869 when the railroad was completed and non-Mormons began to settle in Utah, often to exploit the mineral wealth that helped transform the city in the late nineteenth century. Young maintained that mining was a godless pursuit, so the Mormons made little from those ventures. Meanwhile, Utah continued to press for statehood but polygamy remained the stumbling block. The Supreme Court ruled the practice to be unconstitutional in 1879; by that time Young had been dead for two years, leaving behind sixteen wives and forty-four children.

Actions continued against the Church until 1890, when it suddenly renounced polygamy, publicly at least, and in 1896 Utah became the forty-fifth state of the Union.

After long periods of economic depression, Utah entered a new age of prosperity in the 1940s, booming during and after World War II. The Mormon Church itself entered the economic mainstream and became a wealthy and powerful institution. The discovery of uranium in 1952 sparked a mineral rush, and the space industry created new prosperity. Today, sixty-five percent of the population of Utah are Mormons; and while much of Salt Lake City's architectural heritage has been destroyed by new development, enough remains to attract their brethren from around the world.

PILGRIMS TO THE GREAT SALT LAKE

Present-day pilgrims to Salt Lake City mostly want to tread in the footsteps of their forbears. The truly intrepid pilgrim will attempt to follow part or even all of the Mormon Pioneer Trail, which begins in Nauvoo, Illinois, and winds through Iowa, Nebraska, and Wyoming before reaching Utah

The memorial in Temple Square to Brigham Young, with the names below of all the original pioneers. Salt Lake City's central district retains the layout Young drew up from the plan Joseph Smith devised in 1833 for the true City of Zion.

ABOVE: *One of the world's most celebrated choirs singing in its Salt Lake City home: the Mormon Tabernacle Choir, more than three hundred strong, and in full voice.*

thirteen hundred miles later. In 1997, many re-enactments of the wagon trails took place to celebrate the 150th anniversary of the original pio-neers' reaching their goal. Many of these original few hundred travelers of 1847 had died along the way. They had set out in groups and on a variety of routes, some spending the winter in Kanesville, Iowa, others in Omaha, before they joined forces in Fremont, Nebraska. Military-style discipline kept the party together, and the clerk left messages and

PIONEER PATHS

When they arrive in Utah, many contemporary pilgrims visit Emigration Canyon (now in the Pioneer Trail State Park), through which the original band of Mormons traveled. But what most come to see is Temple Square in Salt Lake City, the ten-acre center of the Mormon faith, bounded by a wall sixteen feet (five meters) high. The confines may be forbidding, but inside is a garden sanctuary and an architectural fantasy land. Dominating everything are the six tall spires of the gray granite Mormon Temple, designed by Brigham Young's brother-in-law Truman Angell, which took forty years to build after the first sod was turned in 1853. On top of the tallest tower, over two hundred feet (sixty-five meters) high, stands a statue of the angel Moroni who delivered to Joseph Smith the gold tablets on which the Book of Mormon had been inscribed, which Smith found at Palmyra, New York in 1822.

Like all Mormon temples, it is open only to practicing Mormons. The Assembly Hall replaced both the original green bower and the original Tabernacle. The vast auditorium that is the present Tabernacle was begun in 1867; it is known around the world for its fine acoustics and for the 325-voice Mormon Tabernacle Choir.

The Church maintains museums, memorials to the pioneers, early houses, and visitor centers in and around the Square. But for many visitors, the primary destination is the archive center. The Family History Library, the world's largest center for genealogical research, is open to all. Genealogy is a mainstay of Mormonism because of the belief that the entire family unit, ancestors included, remains together after death. It is therefore a sacred duty for Mormons to discover as much as possible about their ancestors in order to incorporate them into the scheme; for many Mormon pilgrims to Salt Lake City, their ancestors and their family past are quite as important as the religious historical sites.

marker posts with letters for the pilgrims who were to follow all along the route. Some of these posts, such as the one at Fremont, have now been re-erected to commemorate the pioneers, who—in horse-drawn wagons and even handcarts—blazed the trail westward that modern pilgrims arrive in air-conditioned automobiles to see

The exhilarating moment of arrival, when a weary pilgrim has crossed the mountains and the plains to reach the goal of the city of St. James, Santiago de Compostela, and can exclaim Montjoie! *(My joy!).*

JOURNEY EIGHTEEN

Santiago de Compostela

THE HISTORY OF THE PILGRIMAGE to the shrine of St. James ("the Great") is a story of mystery and spirituality combined with greed, opportunism, and propaganda. The Way of St. James, the ancient pilgrim road that has been trodden for over a thousand years, crosses the Iberian peninsula's northern breadth for almost five hundred miles (eight hundred kilometers) from the heights of the Pyrenees to the wild and wet landscape of Galicia.

UNITED KINGDOM

Dover

BELGIUM

Paris

FRANCE

Tours

Nevers

Poitou

Saintes
Blaye
Limoges

Finistere
Santiago de
Compostela
BAY OF BISCAY
Bordeaux

GALICIA

PYRENEES

Toulouse
St. Gilles
Arles
Marseilles
MONACO

PORTUGAL

Madrid

SPAIN

At Santiago de Compostela in the far west of Spain, the remains of St. James—one of the sons of Zebedee and Mary Salome, and a cousin of Jesus—are said to lie. After Jerusalem and Rome, *Santiago*—Spanish for "St. James"—is the most venerated Christian pilgrimage site.

THE ARDUOUS TREK

In the summer, thousands of pilgrims follow the ancient pilgrimage route, often on foot. For many, the draw is the journey itself rather than the saint who lies at the end. It is a spiritual equivalent of extreme sports; bungee jumping for the soul. In winter, only the most foolhardy and devout would contemplate the journey. Avoiding the mountains

BELOW: *Pilgrims bearing crosses kneel in prayer at Roncesvalles, the Pyrenean pass close to the battlefield where heroic Roland was slain. The revival of the long-distance walking pilgrimage to Santiago de Compostela has been a remarkable modern religious phenomenon.*

on the route is impossible, especially to the west of León and Astorga—the final endurance test for walkers whether in the heat of the summer months or in the snows that last well into spring. For the less hardy, there is a second route to the north that runs along the foothills of the Cantabrian mountains, although the Picos de Europa form another mountain barrier that has to be crossed. But the trek is rewarded by breathtaking views.

The journey was and is a spiritual cleansing, its spirituality heightened by the arduous and, in the past, dangerous, journey to the site. For a thousand years, the route to Santiago de Compostela has inspired this prayer asking God to protect the pilgrim along the way:

Be for him a companion on the march, a guide at the crossroads. Give him strength when he is weak, defense in the midst of danger, shelter along the route, shade from the sun, light in the darkness, solace in moments of discouragement and firmness in his purpose.

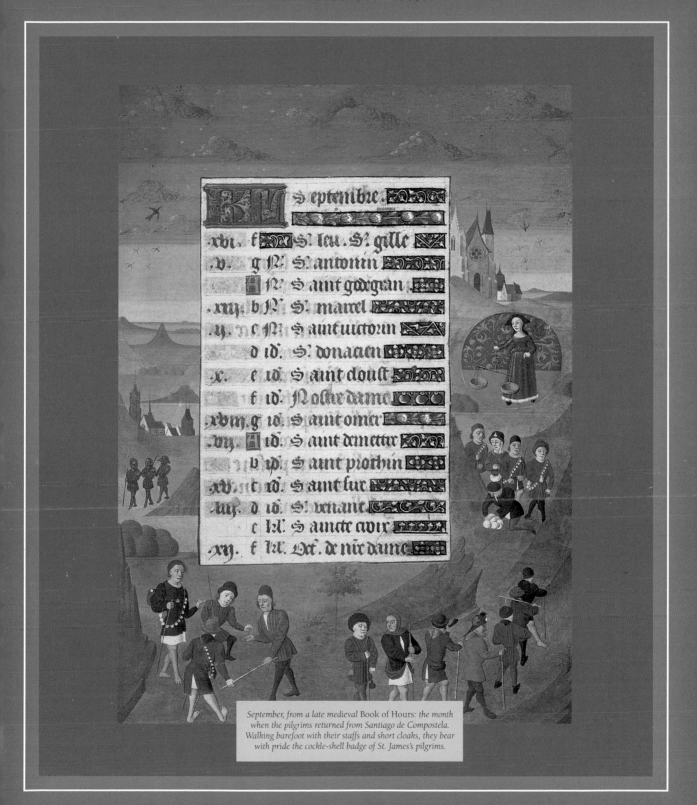

September, from a late medieval Book of Hours: the month when the pilgrims returned from Santiago de Compostela. Walking barefoot with their staffs and short cloaks, they bear with pride the cockle-shell badge of St. James's pilgrims.

The story of how St. James's body came to be in Spain is the subject of legends with no scriptural basis. James had come to Spain to preach the gospel then returned to Jerusalem where he was beheaded in AD 44. His body miraculously returned to Spain, arriving in a stone coffin at a small Galician port called Iris Flavia. Centuries later, in 814, a celestial light drew Bishop Theodomir to the cave where the martyred saint's body had been concealed. Nearby Compostela was chosen as the place where his bones would be buried. Before long, the cult of the gentle saint would help the long process of liberating the Spaniards from their Muslim Moorish masters.

ST. JAMES THE MOOR SLAYER

The Moors had occupied much of Iberia since the early eighth century AD. Entering into a holy war, or *jihad*, the Moors went into battle in the confident belief that Allah sanctioned their endeavor and that they were under the protection of Muhammad (Mohamed), his Prophet. The Christians therefore looked to their chosen protector, *Santiago el Matamoros* —"St. James the Moor Slayer"—who is said to have first appeared on his white horse at the battle of Clavijo in 844. No matter, perhaps, that there is no historical evidence that such a battle ever took place. The crusade against Islamic forces in Spain became as crucial, and fanatical, as the crusades to rescue Jerusalem and the holy places of Palestine from their hands.

Over time, the cult of St. James has acquired many different attributes. The sign of both the saint and the pilgrim is a scallop shell—a sign of the sea and of Cape Finisterre (Land's End.) It is also a

RIGHT: The ancient eleventh-century bridge at Punta La Reina, built on the orders of the Queen of Navarre to ease the passage of pilgrims to Santiago de Compostela, has eased pilgrims' journeys ever since.

ABOVE: Tombs of the Knights of St. James, fifteenth-century fighters for Catholic Spain against the last of the Moors, in the city of Spain's patron, Santiago Matamoros, St. James the Moor Slayer.

traditional symbol of death, used in Roman times to decorate tombs, and at the same time a symbol of sexuality and life, qualities associated with the Greek goddess Aphrodite (later identified by the Romans as Venus). The Milky Way, the clearly visible ribbon of stars in the night sky, was traditionally called St. James's Way, and was supposed to have guided Charlemagne, King of the Franks and Holy Roman Emperor, west to the apostle's tomb.

The legends surrounding the cult of St. James are often far fetched and contradictory. *Compostela* may not have meant "field of stars" as people generally supposed; in reality the place name has the same root as the English word "compost," since the site was an ancient burial ground dating back to the Romans and beyond. It is surely significant that the saint's shrine is not far from the coast at the edge of the then-known world, Finisterre, a place that almost certainly attracted travelers and devotees from prehistory. The Neolithic- and Bronze-Age history of Europe is filled with stones and sacred places that drew people from far away.

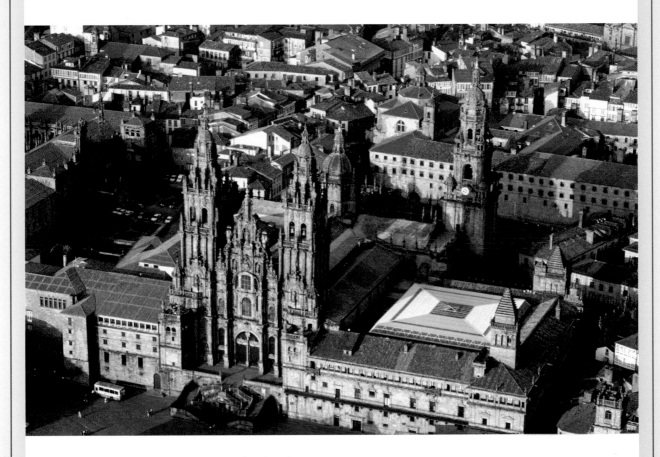

Santiago de Compostela may therefore be a descendant of a more ancient tradition than the post-Dark-Age Christian Church. The summit of Mount Irago, for instance, bears a cross on top of a pole. Traditionally, pilgrims place a stone at the base, praying for a safe journey through the last, wild stretch—an action harking back to prehistory.

THE WAY OF ST. JAMES

The Way is in reality many ways that all finally join together in eastern Spain to make the *Camino Francés* (French Road)—the final, triumphant and

ABOVE: The cathedral church of Santiago, the goal of pilgrims who have followed the Way of St. James. A great Romanesque church is encased within this elaborate baroque structure, with some of the finest sculptures to survive from the early Middle Ages.

wearying approach to Santiago de Compostela. Over ten thousand people a year still follow the Way of St. James as accredited pilgrims, with their *compostellana* (pilgrim's passport) a document the pilgrim is supposed to have stamped by the local priest in each town to verify the progress along the route. The custom of a pilgrim's passport survives from the medieval heyday of the Way, when such documents were worth vast sums in that they con-

ABOVE: *On St. James's Day, when the saint's remains are exhibited in a silver casket, the city is usually filled to overflowing. Pilgrims who have made their way over the hills and mountains are joined by many more who will have come by more comfortable modes of transportation.*

ferred an indulgence on the owner— guaranteed time off from suffering in Purgatory, the halfway house to Heaven.

Along the Way stood the shrines of many saints, and they all helped concentrate the spiritual power and the prayer that funneled through the mountain passes and into Iberia. The Via Tolosana, for pilgrims from Italy and Provence, began at Arles, passed through the towns of St. Gilles and Toulouse—both the sites of significant pilgrimage shrines themselves—and continued on via the Somport Pass into Spain. The Via Podiensis carried pilgrims from Burgundy and Germany. It too had shrines: Le Puy with its miraculous Virgin and the shrine of St. Foy at Conques. This route crossed the

Pyrenees by the Port de Cize. The Via Lemosina began by crossing the Loire at Nevers and passed the shrines of St. Leonard and St. Martial of Limoges, before heading for Ostabat and the mountains. Finally, the Via Turonensis, which was probably the greatest of these main arteries, brought pilgrims from England and throughout northern France. They traveled via Tours and the tomb of St. Martin, through Poitou, Saintes, Blaye—where Charlemagne's heroic martyr Roland was buried—and Bordeaux, before the long haul to Ostabat and over the Pyrenees at the Valcarlos Pass.

The two Pyrenees-crossing routes meet at the Navarre town of Puente la Reina de Jaca. Most pilgrims pass Roncesvalles where, in 778, Charlemagne—not yet, but soon to be Holy Roman Emperor—suffered a great defeat at the hands of Basque forces as his army returned from a seven-year campaign against the Moors. Roland

and all his forces were cut down. The twelfth-century *Chanson de Roland* (in which the Basques became "Saracens") was an epic retelling of the story that resonates still in the European mind.

Guarded by saints, the Way has always been the site of miracles. Most charmingly, a cock and a hen still live in one of the most glorious hen coops in creation, set high above the altar at the cathedral church of Santo Domingo de la Calzada, as reminders of one legend that has accreted to the Way. The story goes that a young pilgrim shunned the amorous advances of a maidservant, and out of pique she then denounced him as a thief, for which he was hanged. But the young man survived execution through the good offices of St. James. When the magistrate refused to believe it, saying the victim was no more alive than the roasted fowls on his table, the cock and the hen sprang up and began to crow and cluck to prove the point.

ABOVE: The casket containing the supposed remains of St. James is housed beneath the altar of the cathedral. Set above is a huge silver head, itself almost a thousand years old, representing St. James.

PILGRIMAGE REVIVAL

At times the Way of St. James follows the main roads, where pilgrims are overtaken by speeding vehicles. Elsewhere, the ancient path diverges from roads and crosses pasture, woods, and marshes. Guidebooks and detailed maps are published in English and in most European languages to aid the walker. Yellow markers are painted on trees, bridges, gates, and even stones, although these markers often disappear at crucial junctures of the journey. In spite of the long, arduous trek to Santiago de Compostela, the supporters of the Way of St. James worldwide have contributed to a pilgrimage revival that has given rise to the establishment of a new hostel in the Bierzo mountains.

All along the route are buildings that reflect the piety and the wealth the pilgrim Way has generated: the great Gothic cathedrals of Burgos, Pamplona, and León; the monastery of San Juan de la Peña; and the hermitage of San Juan de Ortega, built with the saint's own hands. Pilgrims find accommodations in the hospital church at Eunate, the Hospital del Rey at Las Huelgas, and the Hostal de San Marcos near San Isidoro. And everywhere is the sign of the scallop shell and the figure of St. James in his many guises —wise apostle, gentle pilgrim, and fierce Moor Slayer.

REACHING SANTIAGO

A somewhat ludicrous modern statue of a pilgrim now stands at the vantage point where pilgrims obtain their first glimpse of Santiago de Compostela itself, vying with each other to see the sacred city and be the first to utter the traditional pilgrim's cry, *Montjoie!* ("My joy!"). Santiago de Compostela is still one of the most beautiful and best-preserved of all Spanish cities, a warren of streets paved in granite and frequently glistening in the rain, passing the last and grandest of the pilgrims' hostels to the cathedral and shrine itself.

Leaving the relative solitude of the route may come as a shock to the pilgrim as he or she enters the teeming throng gathered at Santiago de Compostela. There, tourists jostle in hordes, especially close to the feast day of St. James on July 25. The twelfth-century Portico de la Gloria, the great entrance portal carved by Master Mateo, is crammed with sculpture: Christ, apostles, prophets, and a heavenly host of angels and saints, ranks of musicians, the tree of Jesse and the Last Judgment. Rising above all this on the portico's central column is the figure of Santiago, St. James himself. The final act in any pilgrim's progress before entering the cathedral shrine is to bow before the saint's image and place a hand

on this column. Countless hands over the centuries have worn smooth hollows into the stone.

A predominantly baroque exterior encases the Romanesque cathedral, and at the nave crossing hangs one of Santiago's most famous features, the *Botafumeiro*, a vast incense-filled censer swung on ropes by teams of men on high days and holy days —part theatrical excess, part devotional intensity. The ancient pilgrim song *Dum pater familias*, preserved in the cathedral library in the twelfth-century *Codex Calixtinus* but dating from well before that, celebrates the apostle and martyr.

Primus ex apostolis
Martir Ilherosolimis
Iacobus egregio sacer est martirio.

Iacobi Gallecia Opem rogat piam
Glebae cuius gloria dat insignem.
Uiarn: ut precum, frequentia
Cantet melodiam.
Herru Sanctiagu, Got Sanctiagu
E ultreia, esus eia.

Deus aia nos.
Primus ex apostolis

First of the apostles
martyred in Jerusalem,
James, sanctified by special martyrdom.

Galicia asks for James's holy power:
his glory constitutes a signpost to the land—
even now—which therefore chants in prayer
frequently and tunefully.
Great St. James, benficent St. James,
From afar off, and with us here.

God assist us.
First of the apostles

Inside the cathedral, as on the long route to get there, images of St. James are everywhere. The final and most splendid figure of the saint, set above the high altar, is clothed in silver and gold and studded with jewels. The saint's supposed remains themselves lie in a silver casket in the crypt beneath— the pilgrim's ultimate goal.

But are St. James's bones really there? And if not, does it really matter? As one modern pilgrim expressed it, the bones—whatever their actual provenance—have been "imbued with sanctity and importance through the pain of the tens of millions of pilgrims throughout the ages."

The historical and spiritual importance of the Way of St. James is beyond dispute. Untold millions followed it in the course of the Middle Ages— from popes to paupers—braving exhaustion, disease, attack, robbery, and fraud. It was a cosmopolitan stream about which Goethe was to write, "Europe was formed journeying to Compostela." Even in the eighteenth and nineteenth centuries, when the tradition of pilgrimage fell into serious decline, sufficient devotion remained to inspire the building and rebuilding of churches, monasteries, and hostels, of which the great baroque cathedral at Santiago de Compostela itself is the finest example. The revival of the tradition during the twentieth century has seen a shift: If the city is still the destination, now the spiritual privilege of the journey itself is the justification for most modern pilgrims who walk, bicycle, or ride the Way of St. James—the great Milky Way on earth—to Santiago de Compostela.

RIGHT: *Over the intervening centuries, the hands of pilgrims have worn almost smooth the carved column at the entrance to the cathedral, the great Romanesque sculptural ensemble of the Portico de la Gloria.*

Throughout the year, pilgrims from West Bengal throng the pilgrim center of Tarekeswar. There they honor Shiva in the form of Baba Taraknath, bringing water from the holy Ganges and satisfying the deity's sweet tooth with appropriate gifts.

JOURNEY NINETEEN

Tarekeswar

THE THIRD-LARGEST INDUSTRY in the town of Tarekeswar in West Bengal, one of India's most populous states, is candymaking. Not that the inhabitants have a particularly sweet tooth—no sweeter than have other Indians—but the god in their temple does. Pilgrims to the temple of Shiva, one of the principal gods of Hinduism, usually bear sweets among their offerings at the shrine. These pilgrims come all year round, to be taken in hand by local guides who act as intermediaries in finding overnight accommodations, buying candies and flowers for the god, organizing the haircuts, and applying the sacred motifs that are all part of the ritual.

ABOVE: *The sacred lingam, the stylized phallus that is one of the characteristic symbols within Shiva's temples. Tarekeswar grew around the spot where a miraculous and sacred stone appeared.*

Shiva is a god of many contrasts presiding over good and evil, fertility and asceticism, and creation and destruction. Most people come to his shrine at Tarekeswar because it is an appropriate way to behave and because it stores up merit for later life and later lives. A few come because they hope the deity will give them help, usually relief from a medical condition. While Tarekeswar may not be the most famous or busiest shrine center in modern India (although it is the busiest in the region), the rituals and practices there go to the heart of Hindu life and observance.

PILGRIM TRAINS

Every hour, a train leaves Calcutta's bustling main Howrah station for Tarekeswar, at the end of a branch line some twenty miles (thirty-two kilometers) and an hour's ride to the west. Alongside the businesspeople, students, farmers, and traders on this train is another sort of traveler. Small groups of well-dressed families sit perched on their seats,

eager with anticipation, their neatness and demeanor in contrast to the other passengers'. The men in these groups all wear white, a fine linen *dhoti* (loincloth) and a well-pressed shirt. The women's saris are colorful and carefully ironed. In the center of their foreheads is an immaculate red dot. They may be accompanied by an elderly widowed relation, dressed in the white of mourning, and by children kept firmly in check. Among the peddlers on the train offering tea, snacks, and toys are incense sellers who target these small groups. The wrappers of the incense sticks bear an image of the god to whose shrine these devout Hindus are traveling—Shiva, or, as his alter ego is called at Tarekeswar, Baba Taraknath.

Traveling to sacred places is a mainstream activity for all but the lowest-caste Hindus. West Bengal is centered on Calcutta and the delta of the River

BELOW: Pitchers of water being brought from the holy river Ganges. Although Tarekeswar is not itself on the Ganges, it lies close to its delta and claims supernatural connection to Benares (Varanasi), the most sacred of all India's cities on the river's banks.

Ganges, but the principal pilgrimage sites like Tarekeswar are located away from major centers of population. Only a minority of pilgrims travel from other parts of India, coming especially to bathe where the Ganges flows into the Bay of Bengal. By the same token, Bengalis are usually very well represented among pilgrims at the larger sites that draw people from all over India: Benares (Varanasi), Hardwar, Mathura, Puri, or the Kumbh Mela (see pages 8–19).

The people and priests of Tarekeswar often refer to their place as *Gupta Varanasi* (hidden Benares,) claiming an identity between the great national pilgrimage site and this lesser one. The most devout

pilgrims carry water on foot from the Ganges to Tarekeswar, and the shrine's phallus or *lingam*, with its immeasurable length beneath the ground, is—they claim—linked to the one in Shiva's shrine located at Benares.

THE LORD SHIVA AND HIS MANIFESTATIONS

At first sight, the aspects of religious life in the region appear complex to the point of bewilderment. There are thousands of deities, hundreds of forms of personal ritual, and dozens of scriptural texts. Some sense of order emerges in the pantheon of deities: every god has many manifestations and forms, from Brahma himself through the two great gods Vishnu and Shiva, down through other deities and semi-deities.

BELOW: Shiva's lingam—sacred representation of a phallus—is the focus of veneration in all temples devoted to him and his various manifestations, including Baba Taraknath. A ritual of offerings and bathing the lingam is part of every Shiva temple's daily observance.

ABOVE: *Varanasi is the Hindu eternal city on the sacred Ganges River. Tarekeswar—known to some as Gupta or hidden Varanasi—has an intense and mystical link to it from almost half a continent away.*

Shiva is believed to be present in his temples. He is held to be a protector of his devotees, especially of ascetics and holy men, and his shrines are particularly busy. Shiva is worshipped in a variety of aspects, "personalities," and forms—the most common being the phallic lingam stylized almost beyond recognition. In India, pilgrims may visit twelve of these preeminent linga sites, sixty-eight major shrines, and many other lesser ones. Linga such as the one at Tarekeswar are especially considered holy because—according to myth—they rose up by themselves rather than being man-made.

In his many guises, Shiva is an erotic lover and also an ascetic. He is a warrior and a peasant, a marijuana-smoker and an artist. Associated with serpents and mountains, his particular beast is the bull (although it was through a cow's milk that the sacred site of Tarekeswar was discovered, according to legend). The trident is one of his most common symbols.

FORDING THE STREAM OF LIFE

The Bengali word for a place of pilgrimage is *tirtha*, which literally means "ford through a stream." Its meaning is both literal and metaphorical. On the one hand, most Hindu holy places are connected with water. On the other, Hindus see life itself as a stream in which they are caught in a series of births and deaths. According to karma—the law of moral and spiritual cause and effect—death only initiates the next existence, the conditions of which are determined by one's actions in previous lives. Earning merit—*punya*—is one way of improving prospects in future lives, and the ritual worship of a deity—*puja*—is an important means of earning merit as well as of pleasing the deity. Divinity takes even greater pleasure when the pilgrim joins austerity with worship and offerings: the hardiest walk to Tarekeswar from the River Ganges, some thirty miles (forty-eight kilometers), barefoot.

PLEASING THE GOD

What is now Tarekeswar was once just dense forest. According to legend, one of the two tax collectors for the ruling *nawab* (Moghul ruler) was a cowman named Bharamalla. He owned a cow that had always provided prodigious amounts of milk. Then she stopped. Following her, the concerned cowman discovered she was releasing her milk onto a rounded stone in the ground. Bharamalla ordered this obviously sacred stone to be dug up; but after twelve days of digging, the workmen still had not reached its bottom. Then Shiva appeared to Bharamalla in a dream, saying the phallic stone was his and should be worshipped on that very spot. Accordingly, a temple was built, and the town grew around it. Other stories recount the first healing miracles that took place there, particularly by applying the *caranamarta*, the runoff of the water, milk, and clarified butter used to wash the lingam.

The evidence suggests that the temple was established around AD 1730, and devotees of Baba Taraknath were particularly attracted by the deity's powers to heal. Baba Taraknath has a physical pres-

ence in his temple, and the priests provide his lingam with creature comforts: meals, pipes of tobacco and marijuana, slippers, a blanket on winter nights, baths of oil, milk, and water.

Thousands of pilgrims each day pay for a share of the ritual meal offered to him, one of many fees they are obliged to offer. They also pay for their heads to be shaved and for the right to share in the puja rituals performed by priests or to take away material that has been consecrated. Even greater numbers pour into the town at the main Shiva feasts, especially the Shivaratri in February–March, which also has a two-week-long fair.

AUSTERITY AND HEALING

Most of the pilgrims are *tirtha-jatris*—that is, they are seeking general spiritual well-being. They come principally from Calcutta and the main towns of West Bengal. A minority are *dharna-jatris*, seeking the god's action through the practice of austerities. These men and women are more commonly from the country areas, and many seek relief or a cure for a medical condition. These pilgrims fast for a number of days and sleep in the temple close to the lingam. Then they have instructions revealed to them in a dream, brought by the god himself or a holy man. If they do not follow the instructions given in the dream to the letter they will not receive their cure—although the instructions may themselves involve further tests of endurance or courage, such as finding the item that will promote healing within a bed of snakes.

The many little votive figures of parts of bodies that are preserved in the temple precinct bear witness to the many cures over the centuries these pilgrims have claimed. Even for the majority who do not seek physical aid from Baba Taraknath, they will all have achieved merit from their undertaking and return to their homes spiritually refreshed.

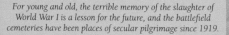

For young and old, the terrible memory of the slaughter of World War I is a lesson for the future, and the battlefield cemeteries have been places of secular pilgrimage since 1919.

JOURNEY TWENTY

The Battlefields of World War 1

A FADING LABEL on a small poppy wreath propped up against a gravestone caused everybody who passed it to stop and ponder, some to weep. The label simply read, "Goodbye, Uncle Frank. This is the last time we will be able to come." Uncle Frank lies in the cemetery on the edge of the little town of Cambrai in northern France, at the scene of the first tank battle in modern warfare. Soldiers from the British and Dominion armies, from the German forces, and from the Russian contingents lie there in peace after the bitter struggles in 1916 that brought death to them all.

UNITED KINGDOM

Thames • London

NETHERLANDS

Ieper • • Passchendaele
• Brussels
Arras •

BELGIUM GERMANY

Seine SOMME

LUXEMBOURG

• Paris

FRANCE

SWITZERLAND

Row upon row, headstone crosses and roses mark millions of graves in the killing fields of northern Europe. The memories of the fallen, like the cemeteries themselves, are maintained and cherished.

At the cemetery near Cambrai are rows of crosses in different styles for each of the nations. Most bear a name, rank, and date; some record no name save, "A soldier of the Great War known unto God." In a modern, secular version of pilgrimage, people still come to honor and wonder in this cemetery with its few thousand graves, just as they do in tiny fieldside enclosures with barely a dozen graves, or in the burial grounds where rows of crosses stretch to the horizon.

THE PITY OF WAR

The First World War of 1914–18 is remembered still, both for the scale of the destruction it caused and for the seeming futility of the struggle. Millions of men were shot, gassed, bayoneted, blown up, or starved to death fighting for advantage over narrow strips of land in northern France and Belgium or in Turkey. Almost as soon as the fighting stopped,

people began journeying to view the scenes for themselves in an act that, although not specifically religious, they self-consciously called a pilgrimage.

More than five million men from the Allied Powers (Britain, France, the U.S., and other nations) and over three million men from the Central Powers (Germany and its partners) died in World War I. Of all the long campaigns on the 450-mile (740-kilometer) length of the Western Front from Switzerland to the English Channel, one that is seared particularly deep into the general consciousness was that fought on the Somme. Losses at the height of an offensive there could be counted in tens of thousands of men per hour. The Road of Remembrance that many pilgrims drive along today, with its poppy-emblazoned signs, crosses

BELOW: The leftovers of war still cling to the landscape. At some battlefield sites, you can smell rust on a damp morning from all the weaponry that still lies just beneath the surface of the ground.

the flat river plain of the Somme for mile after sad mile. The signs point to a seemingly never-ending sequence of memorials and battle sites from the war that was intended to end all wars, but did not.

Although green fields and woods have reclothed the landscape that was once deep, deep mud and trenches, craters excavated by mines still exist as visible reminders of the destruction. At Beaumont-Hamel, some of the trenches themselves have been preserved to memorialize the battle on the Somme, their lines cut in arcing zigzags to prevent a shell from traveling their length. And at hamlets in the area that would otherwise escape notice, swathes of land are given over to the dead. Each nation—French, British, and German—is responsible for tending its own graves, their beautifully manicured order in sharp contrast to the carnage among which all these men died. Rancourt, north of Péronne, for example, is the largest French war cemetery on the Somme. In the German cemetery nearby, where over eleven thousand are buried, the bodies lie four to a grave. The British cemetery is tiny by comparison but, with just ninety-two graves, is one of hundreds of little wayside burial places around this war-saddened lanscape. Books of remembrance at the entrances to these and other war cemeteries record visitors' thoughts, such as: "This must never happen again"; or, "I met the grandfather I never knew for the first time here"; and, "They were just like us."

The legacy of war is evident throughout this region. At Thiepval, south of Arras, is a vast memorial triumphal arch designed by Edwin Lutyens. Visible from a great distance, it is inscribed with the names of men whose bodies were never found —all seventy-three thousand of them. Farther

RIGHT: Time is now smoothing out the sharp contours of the zigzag trenches in which countless men lived, fought, and died in the four long years of fighting on the Western Front.

north, the Belgian army still collects shells from the battlefield near Ieper—or Ypres, but known to British soldiers as '"Wipers"—more than eighty years after the event. In the spring of 1917, a staggering total of nearly five million shells were fired there into a narrow salient on the German front line, one third of which failed to explode in the wet clay. British Field Marshal Haig's chief of staff once wept as he floundered through the mud at Passchendaele in Belgium, "Did we really send men to fight in that?"

PILGRIMAGE TO THE WESTERN FRONT

During the war, British burials were marked by makeshift crosses in small makeshift cemeteries. But afterward, the Imperial (later Commonwealth)

ABOVE and RIGHT: The memories are alive. Tourists are modern-day pilgrims who come to see and wonder in the battlefield cemeteries. They come in the footsteps of those who had originally come to see where their loved ones had fallen between 1914 and 1918.

War Graves Commission, founded in 1917, began to make provision for decent, orderly burial. The practical difficulties of bringing so many bodies back, not to mention the disastrous effect on public morale, led to the decision that men would be buried with their comrades-in-arms close to where they had fallen, in specially constituted cemeteries. Soon, people were coming to see graves that held particular meaning for them. Rudyard Kipling, for one, searched obsessively for his lost son, whose body was never recovered, and Thomas Cook's tour company was organizing visits in August 1919, within a year of the guns falling silent.

"Lest we forget . . ." the phrase may feel overly familiar now,
but for those who were widowed or orphaned by the killing
fields of France and Belgium, there could be no forgetting.

Since most people in Britain did not have Kipling's means and opportunity, the Society of St. Barnabas and the British Legion began offering organized "pilgrimages"—specifically using that term—to the area. They sponsored trips to cemeteries on the Western Front in 1923 and 1927; a trip to Gallipoli in the Dardanelles in 1926; and another trip to the Western Front in 1928. The 1923 pilgrimage to Ieper involved 850 people. In 1928, about ten thousand people made the journey. Visiting a grave or battle site was a substitute for the funeral that had never taken place. One woman who went to Ieper in 1927 wrote, "I picked a poppy near where they told me my boy was last seen."

King George V made his own pilgrimage in 1922. He went in an ordinary army officer's uniform. "I have many times asked myself," said the King-Emperor in whose name so many had fallen, "whether there can be more potent advocates of peace upon earth through the years to come, than this massed multitude of silent witnesses to the desolation of war." He was one of many in the 1920s who hoped these cemeteries might be a beacon for lasting peace. Another great war was to shatter this hope and split the world a mere twenty years later, but the World War I cemeteries remain potent reminders of the dangers, the scale, and the madness of war in any time or place.

PRESENT-DAY PILGRIMS

A child or a grandchild of a fallen soldier may now travel to the cemeteries from Britain, France, Germany, Australia, New Zealand, or Canada, whereas once it would have been a mother, widow, or fiancée. One British writer made the journey in 1990 to the war cemetery at Ieper. Seeing his grandfather's name inscribed on the Menin Gate, he said, "A.T.R. Jones. Those letters had been carved over sixty years ago and never once in all those years had anybody gazed at them with such love and sadness. Somehow those stone letters transferred Alfred from a fading photographic image into a flesh-and-blood man who had lived, fought, and died in a far-off foreign country."

While photographs may fade, memories are not allowed to do so. For almost eighty years at the Menin Gate, a bugler has sounded the Last Post every night without fail at 8:00 P.M. (During the German occupation of Belgium between 1940 and 1944, the ritual was transferred to a military cemetery in Britain; but when the Allied forces regained control of Ieper, the Last Post was immediately heard at the Menin Gate, even though the battle was still raging all around.) Now sometimes great crowds are present to witness the event, especially on or near Armistice Day, November 11. At other times the bugler may stand alone.

Servicemen's and veterans' associations also arrange visits. In Britain, the Old Contemptibles Association—which proudly takes its name from the Kaiser's reported remark that the British soldiery were "a contemptible little army"—organized an annual pilgrimage in August from 1924 until 1974. The surviving veterans on these trips wished both to honor their dead comrades and to make sense for themselves of what they had experienced. After 1974, most were too infirm to make the long journey. And the Australia and New Zealand Army Corps (ANZAC) still sponsors pilgrimages to honor the fallen from these new nations who had come to fight in the imperial cause.

As a recent parallel, the Vietnam War memorial in Washington, D.C., graphically stands in similar recognition of the devastating experience and loss of combat. No graves are there, but column after column of names record the dead, and visitors bring makeshift memorials—a pair of army boots, a flag, a scribbled message—to honor and remember them.

FROM SAINTS TO HEROES

In the 1990s, the numbers of inquiries to the Commonwealth War Graves Commission about particular grave sites increased to twenty times what they were in the mid-1960s. At that time, no commercial companies offered tours and pilgrimages to these sites; now perhaps a dozen companies exist in Britain and a few in other parts of the world, notably Australia and New Zealand. In 1985, the British government instituted a substantial subsidy so that the widows who had not yet visited the grave sites of their men killed in World War I or II could do so.

Following the example of the United States, the British government now brings the bodies of British soldiers home for burial. Hence, the war cemeteries commemorating those who died in 1914–1918 and 1939–1945—with their rows of simple white crosses—have become a historical phenomenon unique to the twentieth century.

But while those who visit them may be motivated by curiosity and a sense of history, many are indeed pilgrims seeking some personal, psychological, and even spiritual fulfillment. The men resting in these battlefield cemeteries have become heroes, replacing in cultural consciousness the saints whose remains were visited in earlier centuries. Many will dispute the cause for which they died, but few will deny their heroic status. Nobody goes to these sites and hopes for miracles, but many hope for some sort of healing or a sense of completion and closure. Religious overtones are everywhere, in graveyard crosses and graveside hymn-singing, but the visitors' experiences are emotional and often intense, whether the graves visited are of family or friends, or neither. We might see these pilgrimages as being on behalf of all people: when modern pilgrims come to mourn a particular loved one or just to wonder at man's inhumanity to man, they also come in hope of the resolution of conflict by violence and to affirm our common humanity. Perhaps Wilfred Owen, one of many great poets inspired by the experiences of the War, expressed it best in his poem "Strange Meeting." He wrote it in 1918 shortly before he too was killed, at the Sambre, only weeks before the armistice. In it a British and a German soldier meet "down some profound dull tunnel" in death and—one hopes—in the peace that stretches beyond.

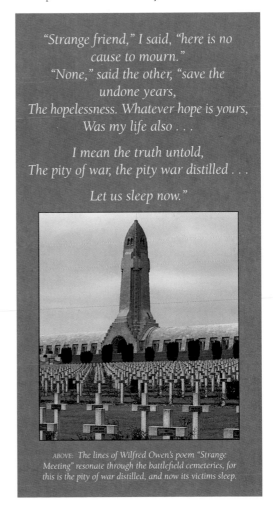

"Strange friend," I said, "here is no cause to mourn."
"None," said the other, "save the undone years,
The hopelessness. Whatever hope is yours,
Was my life also . . .

I mean the truth untold,
The pity of war, the pity war distilled . . .

Let us sleep now."

ABOVE: *The lines of Wilfred Owen's poem "Strange Meeting" resonate through the battlefield cemeteries, for this is the pity of war distilled, and now its victims sleep.*

To be a pilgrim

Each religion has some ideal of pilgrimage: a "true" pilgrim will be transformed by the experience and will accept it with appropriate reverence and decorum, or with appropriate ecstasy. In truth, there are probably just as many responses of pilgrims to what they do and see as there are pilgrims. What satisfaction does a Zuñi rain dancer get from making his own physical and spiritual journey? With what hope does a sick person travel to Lourdes, and with what feelings does he or she return, uncured? How does a Muslim at Mecca feel at not being able to get anywhere near the sacred stone? How does a pilgrim to the Holy Sepulcher in Jerusalem feel at being prevented from gaining access to the site of the tomb, and how do Protestant pilgrims to Jerusalem regard this tomb rather than the alternative site of the tomb they come to venerate? Do those who trudge their weary way to Santiago de Compostela feel that arriving at the destination is anticlimatic? Or is it a transcendent experience? How important is it to pilgrims that countless millions have passed a particular way before them? How necessary is it to believe absolutely in what they are doing, and do they hope to gain faith through their action?

The souvenirs of pilgrimage—amulets, relics, and so on—help to reconstruct the sacred journey in the imagination so that, long after the trip is over, a pilgrim may remember what happened on the way to or at the site. For those who have not made a pilgrimage, objects themselves provide a link with a sacred goal. The testimonies of pilgrims, their stories, texts, and prayers, all inspire future generations. The common link is that the process of going on pilgrimage and being a pilgrim reinforces what people think they are. It also changes them—sometimes in small ways, occasionally in big ways.

In the flux of human history over the past few thousand years, pilgrimage has been one of the most colorful and dramatic constants for enlivening the spirit and deepening the soul.

Bibliography

Many books, guides, articles, and websites have been useful in writing this book. Among the great variety of works consulted are:

Richard Barber. *Pilgrimages*. Woodbridge: Boydell Press, 1991.

Bhardwaj, S. M. et al., ed. *Pilgrimage in the Old and New Worlds*. Berlin, 1994.

Coleman, Simon, and John Elsner. *Pilgrimage Past and Present in World Religions*. Cambridge, Mass.: Harvard University Press, 1995.

Dyer, Geoff. *The Missing of the Somme*. London, 1994.

Eade, John, and Michael Sallnow, eds. *Contesting the Sacred: The Anthropology of Christian Pilgrimage*. London: Routledge, 1991.

Guellouz, Azzedine, and Abdelaziz Frikha. *Mecca: The Muslim Pilgrimage*. New York: Paddington Press, 1979.

Harris, Ruth, *Lourdes: Body and Spirit in the Secular Age* New York: Viking, 1999.

Jha, Makhan, ed. *Dimensions of Pilgrimage*. New Delhi, Inter-India Publications, 1985.

——. *Social Anthropology of Pilgrimage*. New Delhi, Inter-India Publications, 1991.

Johnson, Russell, and Kerry Moran *The Sacred Mountain of Tibet: On Pilgrimage to Kailas*. Rochester, Vt.: Park Street Press, 1989.

Madan, T. N. *Religion in India*. Delhi; New York: Oxford University Press, 1991.

Morinis, Alan, ed. *Sacred Journeys: The Anthropology of Pilgrimage*. Westport, Conn.: Greenwood Press, 1992.

Munro, Eleanor. *On Glory Roads: A Pilgrim's Book about Pilgrimage*. New York: Thames and Hudson, 1987.

Nolan, Mary Lee, and Sidney Nolan. *Christian Pilgrimage in Modern Western Europe*. Chapel Hill: University of North Carolina Press, 1989.

Peters, F. E. *Jerusalem and Mecca: The Typology of the Holy City in the Near East*. New York: New York University Press, 1986.

Poole, Stafford, *Our Lady of Guadalupe: The Origins and Sources of a Mexican National Symbol*. Tucson: University of Arizona Press,1998.

Reader, Ian, and Tony Walter, eds. *Pilgrimage in Popular Culture*. Basingstoke: Macmillan, 1993.

Robinson, Martin. *Sacred Places, Pilgrim Paths: An Anthology of Pilgrimage*. London: HarperCollins, 1997.

Shrady, Nicholas. *Sacred Roads: Adventures from the Pilgrimage Trail*. San Francisco: HarperSanFrancisco, 1999.

Statler, Oliver. *Japanese Pilgrimage*. New York: Morrow, 1983.

Turner, Victor, and Edith Turner. *Image and Pilgrimage in Christian Culture*. New York: Colombia University Press, 1978.

The author would like to thank Sophie Collins and The Ivy Press for the invitation to think and to write about pilgrimage and for seeing the project through, Simon de Quincey, Sadhbh and Piotr Szczesny, José Luís Cano Ruiz, Julie Wheelwright and his wife Nicola.

The quote from *The Way of the White Clouds* by Lama Anagerika Govinda, published by Rider. Reprinted by permission of The Random House Group Ltd.

PICTURE ACKNOWLEDGMENTS

AKG, London
123, 160 Gilles Mermet, 169, 171, 187 Eric Lessing

CORBIS
6 Janez Skok, 10/11 Chris Lisle, 13 Jeremy Horner, 17, 18 Chris Lisle, 22/3 Michael Freeman, 24/25 Chris Lisle, 27 Eye Ubiquitous, 28 Wolfgang Kaehler, 30 Danny Lehman, 31 David Muench, 32 Richard Cummins, 34/5 Craig Aurness, 36 David and Peter Turnley, 38 Dave G. Houser, 40 David and Peter Turnley, 42 Owen Franken, 48 Peter Wilson, 52/3 Tony Arruza, 54 Bettman, 55 Tim Page, 57 Hans Georg Roth, 58, 60 Danny Lehman, 61 Charles and Josette Lenars, 62 Danny Lehman, 64 Sergio Dorantes, 66 Annie Griffith Belt, 68/9 Richard T. Nowitz, 70 Annie Griffith Belt, 71 Ted Spiegel, 73 David H. Wells, 74 Paul A. Souders, 75 Annie Griffith Belt, 78, 81, 82/3, 85 Tim Page, 86 Chris Lisle, 88 Craig Lovell, 89 Nik Wheeler, 91 Michael S. Yamashita, 93 Robert Holmes, 94 Farrell Grehan, 97 Jonathan Blair, 98 Lake County Museum, 100 Robert Estall, 101 Dave G. Houser, 102 Ric Ergenbright, 105 Marc Garanger, 106 Bettmann, 107 Eye Ubiquitous, 152 Kevin Fleming, 124 Galen Rowell, 128/9 David Samuel Robbins, 132 Galen Rowell, 135 Tiziana and Gianni Baldizzone, 142 Vittoriano Rastelli, 144/5 Ted Speigel, 146 Archivio Iconografico, 147 Bettmann, 148 Fluvio Roiter, 149 James L. Amos, 150/1 Vittoriano Rastelli, 152 Kevin Fleming, 157 Lowell Georgia, 162 Nik Wheeler, 164/5, 166 Adam Woolfit, 167 Voz Noticias, 168 Eye Ubiquitous, 172 Ric Ergenbright, 174 M. Jellife, 175 David Samuel Robbins, 176 Brian Vikander, 182, 183, 185 Hulton-Deutsch Collection

HUTCHINSON LIBRARY
80 Jenny Pate, 126/7, 130/1 Jonathan Hope, 133 Pierrette Collomb, 174 M. Jellife

REX FEATURES
8, 12, 14/5, 108, 110/1, 112, 114/5, 119, 120/1, 141, 178, 184

DAVID SOUDEN
50, 51

TRIP/ART DIRECTORS
20 Helene Rogers, 45, 46 J. D. Dallet, 109 B.Gadsby, 114, 116, 118, 127 J. Sweeney, 136, 138, 139, 154, 155, 156, 158/9 Bob Turner, 180/1